THE BIRDSIDE BAPTIST

Also by Joe Neal

Rambling through Arkansas (1974)

Blackberry Heaven (1974)

Arkansas Birds: Their Distribution and Abundance
(with Douglas A. James, 1986)

Birding in the Western Arkansas Ozarks
(with Mike Mlodinow, 1989)

History of Washington County, Arkansas (1989)

*Factors Affecting Breeding Success of
Red-cockaded Woodpeckers in the
Ouachita National Forest, Arkansas* (1992)

Turtles Crossing (2001)

A Western Arkansas Scrapbook (2001)

Birds in Northwestern Arkansas, An Ecological Perspective (2009)

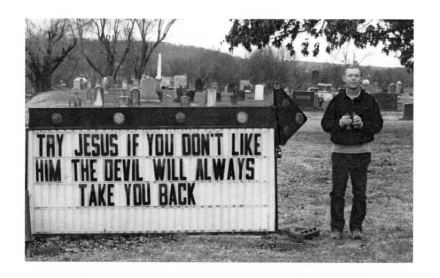

The Birdside Baptist

And Other Ornithological Mysteries

JOSEPH C. NEAL

HALF
ACRE
PRESS
Fayetteville
2010

Copyright © 2010 by Joseph C. Neal

ISBN-13: 978-0-9829455-0-6

All photographs by Joseph C. Neal except where noted
Designed by Liz Lester

Support for this project has been provided by:

Restoring unique Ozark natural communities
to presettlement condition 501(c) (3) non-profit

OERI
104 Skilern
Siloam Springs, AR 72761
479-427-4277

and by:

etchings.org
Richard Stauffacher, artist
3048 Hughmount Road
Fayetteville, AR 72704

Preferred citation:
Neal, Joseph C. 2010. *The Birdside Baptist (And Other Ornithological Mysteries)*.
Half Acre Press, Fayetteville AR. 162 pp.

frontispiece photo: Joe Neal in Prairie Grove on the way to Tenkiller Lake,
January 23, 2010. *Photo by Jacque Brown.*

HALF
ACRE
PRESS
www.halfacrepress.com

CONTENTS

2006

2007

2008

2009

2010

CONTENTS

ACKNOWLEDGMENTS AND DEDICATIONS

This little volume is dedicated to the Birds of Arkansas Discussion List (ARBIRD-L) subscribers, old and new, young and old, Baptist and heathen, and even Methodist (just kidding).

These essays also go out to friends of mine who prefer their ARBIRD-L posts terse: just a couple of words and right to the rare bird, all well displayed on the iPhone. Wordy, opinionated essays on ARBIRD-L don't work that well on the iPhone. That's why god, in his infinite wisdom, gave us the DELETE key.

Many thanks to Ozark Ecological Restoration, Inc. (OERI), and its president and founder, Joe Woolbright of Siloam Springs, Arkansas, for numerous environmentally positive projects in northwestern Arkansas, plus a lot of interesting fun in the field. Joe and OERI generously provided support that encouraged publication of this volume.

Richard Stauffacher, working artist and creator of numerous etchings often featuring natural history in northwestern Arkansas, including birds, has generously hosted several of my writing projects on his web site, etchings.org.

Thanks to all of you out there who have given your Sundays to join me for divine ornithological services at Birdside Baptist, in the field.

Finally, book designer and publisher, Liz Lester, encouraged me to go beyond my original plan of a simple online project and make it a real book, with lots of images to go with the text. It is because of her encouragement that we are here now.

Great Egrets at Centerton on August 11, 2004. This bird appeared headed for extinction a century ago because of killing for its gorgeous nuptial feathers. It was saved by public outcry and became a symbol of the National Audubon Society. It is today a common migrant and nests in low numbers in northwestern Arkansas.

INTRODUCTION

If you are looking for an explanation for the somewhat weird title, check out my entry for August 22, 2009. When my sister misses Sunday morning services and instead enjoys preaching on TV, she refers to this as attending "bedside Baptist." Out birding on a Sunday morning, I guess we may claim to be attending "birdside Baptist." I have attended many such services over the years, some described in this essay collection.

In terms of trying to understand where I am coming from in these essays, it will help if you were a kid growing up in Fort Smith, Arkansas, in the 1950s and attending five church services a week, always wearing shiny black shoes that pinched growing toes and a tie that was meant to show how serious Hazel and Grover Ray Neal's son was supposed to be about Jesus business. But, maybe some of this will make sense, even if your own growing up was somewhat deficient in suitably strong doses of Christianity, Arkansas style.

Over the years more than four hundred Arkansans, plus others from out of state (and occasionally from other countries), have posted their daily bird records, observations of life touching on birds, and passions about politics, butterflies, and what have you on the ARBIRD-L. It's a birder's town meeting well attended by Arkansans from all walks of life, rich and poor, old and young.

My old friend and birding companion, Dr. Kimberly G. Smith of the Department of Biological Sciences at the University of Arkansas-Fayetteville, is the "owner" of the discussion list, which is hosted by servers on campus. Generally he lets us post whatever we want as long it has some relevance to birds in Arkansas. It's an economical way of connecting taxpayers who support the university with ornithological pursuits all over the Great State of Arkansas. But sometimes Kim must reject or at least edit potentially controversial references to subjects associated with our modern so-called "culture wars" (e.g., religion). Paying close attention to such realities is one of the problems of living here, on the Buckle of the Bible Belt. You never know when you are going to offend someone, from the "left" or the "right." It makes sense to keep a public discussion associated with the U of A out of the middle of that dog fight.

I got by with posting to **ARBIRD-L** a welcome for Christian Conservative Birders (July 1, 2009) to go birding with some of us backsliding birders, but I guess that stirred up the hornets. I was one of the first to get stung. My Birdside Baptist posting for August 22, 2009, was heavily edited, down to the bare birds actually. But now I have my sweet revenge: the copy included in this essay collection is restored to its true (?) luster.

I know someone who manages a public list like **ARBIRD-L** has to be concerned about the culture wars. Kim is not the first editor to take a solid whack at my writing in my forty-year toils at the typewriter. Mostly I have benefited from these whacks.

In the essays and reports that follow, you will discover many references to my origins as a Southern Baptist, subspecies *arkansensis,* a part of my heritage that I cherish and value, even if I am not often in the formal pews of Sunday mornings or any of the other sacred days of the week (note to non-Baptists: we call no shows in the pews "backsliding").

As I grew older, I decided that God must have created a heck of a lot more than just brick and mortar churches. I arrived at the settled opinion that we may worship and give thanks just about anywhere in this vast creation. It has to do with how you see it. I often see it through binoculars; hence, my life as a birdside Baptist and backslider.

But back to the **ARBIRD-L**. Only on a few occasions when we've just gone on and on and on about one subject has Kim intervened and told us, "Move on." He was about to pull the plug after numerous angry postings about a cranky radio station's offer for Kill the Woodpecker mugs shortly after the Ivory-billed Woodpecker was rediscovered in 2004. We were all pretty hot about the Kill the Woodpecker deal, even though it was probably a publicity stunt. We **ARBIRDERS** take our woodpeckers seriously! Kim is also the one to remind us not to post anything but words: "Hi, All . . . a friendly reminder that attachments and/or pictures are not allowed on this list . . . Either post pictures off-site and give the address or ask people to contact you directly for a copy . . . Thanks, The Management"—from January 15, 2007.

Kimberly G. Smith in his office in the UA-Fayetteville Department of Biological Sciences in 2010.

I made scattered postings to ARBIRD-L from 2002 to 2004, and with greater regularity thereafter. At times I expanded lists of birds found during field trips into short essays. These essays reflect discoveries and random thoughts while birding in the field: my vista. These short essays reflect what I'm experiencing on the western Arkansas birding frontier, my ornithological vista. Here and there I have edited the posts for clarity. But, for better or for worse, this is mainly the way they went to ARBIRD-L.

It has been a lot of fun to write these essays. I am grateful to Kim for keeping the enterprise going, even though I maintain he is just too hard on us poor Baptists. I am also grateful to a small handful of subscribers who actually took time over the years to read some of these essays as they came out on the list. Your acknowledgment of me as a birder and writer makes it worthwhile. You can't imagine what pleasure your comments have given to me. You inspire me to keep searching and to keep thinking. Thank you so much.

Finally, subscribing to ARBIRD-L is cheap and easy (actually free) and so is unsubscribing, if you become disgusted. The easiest way to start filling up your email box with bulletins from Arkansas's busy and endlessly curious birding community is to go to the home page of Arkansas Audubon Society and tap the link for the bird discussion list. It is all there—quick and easy guide to subscribing.

I actually have more to share here for this introduction, BUT I'm in a rush to get back to my email inbox to see if anyone on ARBIRD-L has yet figured out how to identify those darn vexing immature fall ibises. Glossy? White-faced?

So that's it for now. Welcome one and all—believers and heathens alike—to divine services at Birdside Baptist.

—J. Neal
August 2010

THE BIRDSIDE BAPTIST

American Robin on yaupon shrub at Fayetteville Post Office on Dickson Street, February 15, 2007. Robin flocks crowded shrubs with berries during harsh winter weather.

2002

Lessons from Winter Fields

This year's Fayetteville's Christmas Bird Count (CBC) underscored for me the diverse ecological roles of wetlands—whether obvious ones with water and cattails, or less obvious ones with only endemic Ozark Burrowing Crawfish and migratory birds.

I was thinking about this during the annual Fayetteville Christmas Bird Count held Sunday, December 15, 2002. The Fayetteville count dates back to the 1920s. I have done analysis of the most recent forty years of the count, dating to the early 1960s. Since CBCs are held all over the U.S., plus Canada, Mexico, etc., the data provides a snapshot of where birds are at midwinter.

This year the Clabber Creek bottomlands were searched for wintering birds by my group of three experienced birders (myself, biologist Irene Camargo, and artist Richard Stauffacher) and another headed by Arkansas native and U of A PhD student, Rob Doster. I was responsible for the city-owned Wilson Springs property. Rob covered adjacent Clabber bottomlands including the Razorback golf course and a parcel just east of Salem Road.

Perennial as well as seasonal wetlands in the Clabber Creek bottomlands play an important role in the life cycles of several groups of birds—none of which, unlike Bald Eagles, are household names.

The numbers of Song Sparrows and Swamp Sparrows were especially impressive. These are among the highest numbers EVER found on a Fayetteville CBC. Of course, it was a mild day, and as a result, we could easily find the birds, but the high numbers recorded can also be explained by the quality of the habitat: Clabber's grassy, wet former Tallgrass Prairie habitat is a fine place for these wintering birds.

Le Conte's Sparrow and Sedge Wren are small birds that have always been very hard to find in the Fayetteville area in winter. This was a big year for them here, too, and all were found in the fields along Clabber Creek.

I mention these things because we tend to focus on birds rare and somewhat novel. In focusing on them and their fate, we focus our energies to save their habitat. This is a good impulse, but quality habitat for even more common species is important if these creatures are to avoid the downward slide toward rarity.

What I find interesting is how the birds themselves make selections. They don't worry about how wide a strip of land to save along the creek. They don't carry on debates about whether or not society as we know it will collapse if we don't add another twenty-five jobs or acres of parking lot to the Fayetteville landscape. Their presence in such numbers indicates habitat quality that may not be so obvious to many human observers. They have selected the Wilson Springs bottomland fields as a valuable place. They are waiting on us to catch up to their discovery and selection.

2003

Wilson Springs

I have made several posts to this list concerning the Wilson Springs property near Northwest Arkansas Mall and the University of Arkansas-Fayetteville. You may recall that this public property has nesting season populations of Henslow's Sparrow, Bell's Vireo, Sedge Wren, Painted Bunting, and others. I have networked with American Bird Conservancy (Jane Fitzgerald), Arkansas Audubon Society, Audubon Arkansas, Arkansas Game & Fish, and others about this property and some adjacent land in Clabber Creek bottoms. None of this is "critical" for salvation of these species, but I don't personally know what would be critical, so being the conservative person I am, I decided it was worth starting right at Wilson Springs to protect these birds and other species of highly threatened lowland Tallgrass Prairies. Jane Fitzgerald (who lives in Missouri) asked me what was going on. Andrea Radwell, who has spent years studying and defending the spring itself and its associated wetlands values, asked me what I thought was going on. So here goes my personal view.

As you may recall, as a controversy developed about the future of the Wilson Springs property, our mayor appointed a task force to help him resolve the conflict. The task force, including Sierra Club, U of A, and Chamber of Commerce reps, decided that only about 70 of the 289 acres were really suitable for development, and that most of the rest should get some kind of protection (at least 189 of the total, if my memory serves). The mayor rejected this finding, apparently because he did not believe the ecological values were that great, and because the money on the table was such a big stack. Like every other government entity in this great land of ours, Fayetteville has a budget crisis. He stated

Fledgling Green Heron in Clabber Creek bottomlands at Fayetteville on
August 1, 2004.

that selling this property could generate funds for other parklands—not
a bad idea in some other context. So he went out and found a developer
to buy the whole tract for almost $6 million. That's where things stand
now. It's a logical business decision on the mayor's part.

My friend Don Nelms (who is chairman of the board for Audubon
Arkansas) has apparently worked out an arrangement whereby up to
125 of the most sensitive acres would become part of an Audubon
Nature Center. There seems to be a deal with the new owner on this,
though the swirl goes on at least in part because Sierra Club is holding
the developer's feet to the fire by demanding a new wetlands delineation. I don't know if money has changed hands nor do I have a good feel
about the delineation.

As far as I am personally concerned, if there are Ozark Burrowing
Crawfish on the land in question, it's a wetland. I don't think Congress
in its wisdom mentioned our endemic crawfish, so it may be that the
official delineators may ignore thousands of years of crawfish "wet-

land delineations," migrating Soras, Sedge Wrens, and those American Bitterns I found out there in spring. The crawfish claim about 229 acres of the property in their wetland delineation. I'll have to go with them, since they are the real wetlands experts, according to the big chimneys they build and their explorations by tunneling into the underlying groundwater.

I have not personally "washed my hands" of the situation, but I know I (and many others) did all I could to promote the ecological values of the land. I tried to promote the idea that, like the National Forest where I work, Wilson Springs was "public land" and could be managed as such and not simply for its economic values. This view had traction with some, but did not prevail. In my view, Wilson Springs is a lot like National Forests—it could be managed for multiple uses, including economics; but economics would be just one part of the package.

The main thing I got out of all of this was a nuts and bolts understanding and appreciation for the lowland, seasonal wetland aspects of Tallgrass Prairie and the floral and avian aspects of this community. Wilson Springs has been a lab for me and a graduate course. I've had many enjoyable days birding and botanizing within sight of the NWA Mall and the U of A. I learned a lot about Henslow's Sparrow, Bell's Vireo, Sedge Wren, and others birds of this habitat. I now speak "hydric soils" like the cracker-barrel expert I am. It has greatly increased my understanding of fundamental ecological issues about prairies, springs, and associated wetlands in western Arkansas. It could be that way for many others, too, though this vision is not the one that prevailed. Parts of this vision could be realized in an Audubon Center.

I personally think it's worth a lot more than $6 million, but admittedly I'm thinking what folks are going to say fifty years from now, about all that green space that could have been preserved in the middle of an urban area of one million people. It's like we had a chance to save a version of Central Park in the Ozarks but our mayor—and the views of the many folks he represents in this respect—could not see it that way. Nobody but a few ecowackos consults the Ozark Burrowing Crawfish or the Sedge Wrens—but then that goes without saying.

The mayor won office here with a lot of support from the "green" community; so you can image the disappointment, since it turns out that, while our mayor does have mainstream values about the need to protect the environment and has done several things in office to promote "green" values, he does not take the same views as say, we biologists. By comparison, I guess we are radicals. This does not make him an evil or shallow person in my view. The world needs mayor/politicians and it also, maybe, perhaps, needs mouthy biologists. (Mayors run for office; biologists run from bill collectors). Wilson Springs provides a cautionary tale about political endorsements on one hand and lost opportunities on another. I'd humbly offer the opinion that folks bashing the mayor over this remember that there are many, many folks with less of an interest in the environment than he has, and he has always favored protecting at least part of the wetland at Wilson Springs.

I have personally shifted gears to help Audubon in its efforts to manage Wilson Springs. This will be a worthwhile project and will provide numerous future opportunities for western Arkansas. Ozark Burrowing Crawfish are snapping their claws in support of this idea, though it entails loss of part of their Wilson Springs homeland. Many others are still working on the wetlands issue to insure that, whatever the outcome of all this, the wetlands receive the full protection they deserve, and not just lip service. There are other contentious issues in Fayetteville and a lot of damage being done to streams and wetlands in the name of "Progress."

Ah, Progress. Ah, Holy Grail of Civic Improvement. Without you and your tender mercies, we would still be crouching under the bluff lines and gnawing on acorns.

I hope that the feisty folks who have fought for Wilson Springs will take heart, "gird up their loins" as the Holy Bible puts it, and get ready for whatever lies ahead. It adds an interesting aspect to our civic life, and sometimes we make Progress (gulp) on the environmental front!

Red-cockaded Woodpecker Nesting Season Ouachita NF

JULY

I've been meaning to update our list on what's happened to our Red-cockaded Woodpecker recovery efforts here on the Ouachita National Forest in western AR. The nesting season for 2003 is over and it was excellent overall. It follows excellent years especially in 2001 and 2002. It appears at this point to be a positive trend. That is to say, the Ouachita NF population appears to be growing and it appears it is going to avoid the extirpation (or local extinction) that has been the fate of almost all isolated populations (isolated because of habitat loss and fire suppression) across the bird's range in the Southeastern U.S.

If you combine our efforts on the Ouachita NF with those being made by the State of Oklahoma on the McCurtain Wilderness Area (MWA) in McCurtain County, Oklahoma, it looks like we are on our way to a really wonderful tale of recovery. The MWA is in the eastern Oklahoma region of the Ouachita Mountains. Like the population in the Waldron, Arkansas area (where I work), the MWA RCW population represents a saved remnant with potential to recover as habitat in the western Ouachitas recovers. We know these populations are already in contact, based upon bird banding efforts in both the MWA and the Ouachita NF .

Here are some numbers: The Ouachita NF population had been in a long decline, likely since the original forest was cut off—when all of what is now NF was privately owned—and fires were suppressed. The Forest Service began an accelerated recovery effort in the early 1990s. The population continued to dwindle for several reasons through the mid-1990s, but then began to stabilize.

The low point with fledglings came in 1997, when only 7 young birds left nests in the Waldron area; this compares to 47 in 2003.

The low point with nesting attempts came in 1996, with 11 attempts; there were 26 in 2003.

The low point in the number of active territories came in 1996, with 11; there were 30 by 2003.

Red-cockaded Woodpecker feeding nestlings in the Ouachita
NF on May 31, 2006. These endangered birds are making a
comeback on the Ouachita NF due to an active recovery effort.
The adult bird is banded as part of this effort and the nest is in
an artificial cavity readily accepted for both night roosting and
nesting.

Many things have contributed to what appears to be a turnaround. In a mechanical sense, FS personnel in Texas, Louisiana, and elsewhere have helped by finding young birds that could be moved to the Ouachitas. This provided opportunities for Ouachita birds to find new mates, establish territories, and rear a fresh batch of young birds. It helped overcome some of the genetic problems associated with a long period of isolation. The Ouachita NF has supported efforts to manage and improve habitat suitable for RCWs, as well as other plant and animal species that require this habitat (such as Bachman's Sparrow, Prairie Warbler, etc.). Many people—both within the FS as well as outside— have gone way over the top in their efforts to save this population and to put it on the road to recovery.

Many more things could be listed, but I should say LAST BUT NOT LEAST, RCWs in the Ouachita Mountains have demonstrated resiliency in the face of such incredible and overwhelmingly negative changes in a landscape that once supported them and many other species that are now "rare"—not because of problems with their genes, but because we modified the landscape in a radical way before realizing what we were losing.

Paraphrasing Aldo Leopold, we fortunately saved this part. We may once again see a robust ecosystem based upon this saved part.

Pileated Woodpecker feeding nestlings in a shortleaf pine snag, Ouachita NF, in late May 2006. Pileateds are fairly common in mature forests, especially those with plenty of big dead trees.

2004

Incredible Woodpecker Story

SEPTEMBER

Here's a just absolutely amazing TRUE story involving Red-cockaded Woodpeckers, and the effort to bring them back from the edge of extinction in Arkansas and Louisiana. It involves the Ouachita NF ranger districts in western Arkansas where I help with the RCW recovery effort. Warren Montague, wildlife program manager and leader of the Ouachita NF's RCW recovery effort, provided the following data.

Most of you may already know that RCWs are endangered because of massive (~99%) loss of mature growth pine in the southeastern United States. So much habitat has been lost that normal dispersal of female RCWs has become difficult (do to huge areas with unsuitable habitat). This leads to isolation and eventual extinction of small populations that under former habitat conditions were healthy. But, as it turns out, the will to survive is very strong in this species.

In 1995, Warren and his RCW team banded a juvenile female RCW in Scott County, AR, north of the Parks community. This bird received a permanent metal band on the right leg, plus a color band on the right, and two color bands on the left. Subsequently, this bird "disappeared" from the Ouachita NF. However, Forest Service biologists on the Winn Ranger District in Louisiana, also working on RCW recovery, later spotted this same bird there, approximately 210 AIR miles away! This new Louisiana resident found a mate and nested, and reared several batches of young woodpeckers in the following years.

This event was incredible on several accounts. In the first instance, banding is a lot of work, and the chances that banders would actually find a bird that had flown this far is extremely low—especially when you realize that this is one of the longest known dispersal distances ever recorded for an RCW. But the story just gets better.

Last week, Warren and trainee biologist Jason Nolde were monitoring an RCW cavity that had become suddenly and unexpectedly active in an area of the Ouachita NF north of Parks. Was there an RCW there? They got the band colors, which did not mesh with any in use on the Ouachita NF. Checking in a wider area showed this bird had come . . . from the Winn RD in Louisiana! It was not the original female RCW of 1995 either. Instead, it was her GRANDDAUGHTER!!! This bird had retraced the 210 AIR miles, and taken up residence on the Ouachita NF two miles—yes, that's two miles—from where her grandmother had started life!

The implications for these discoveries are mind boggling. Who says we have all of the answers? The optimist in me says that no matter how much we damage habitat, our fellow creatures retain a will to survive— and to flourish.

The biologist in me notes that the habitat where grandmother started life is being intensively managed on public lands to guarantee that there will be a flourishing population of RCWs in future years. The cluster of trees where the granddaughter returned includes artificial cavities installed by Warren and wildlife tech Keith Piles as part of an effort to make the area more attractive to RCWs.

It sheds fresh light on the sometimes dull and seemingly unproductive days working with RCWs. It suggests we can slowly retrace and improve the situation that lead to endangerment. To me it says we don't have to be victims of the past. Actually and metaphorically, we can recover and move on.

Fish-eating Birds, Bird-killing People

Twenty years ago in Benton County, a father took his two sons out to a hillside above Osage Creek, overlooking a rookery where Great Blue Herons were nesting. He showed them how to shoot the "Blue Cranes" right out of their nests, while sitting in lawn chairs. They killed as many as they could, then came back the next weekend to finish. A neighbor in the area couldn't take any more of it. She made a call, and as a result, an enforcement officer from Arkansas Game & Fish caught them in the act and got fines levied. I salute her courage and civic mindedness in making her call.

The man claimed that fishing was bad because GBHs were wiping out all of the fish in local streams. It's one of the relatively rare cases in which it has been possible to actually catch people doing such things, then to get convictions. I salute AG & F for such valiant efforts and many other efforts on behalf of nongame bird management in Arkansas. Our hunting and nonhunting wildlife-enjoying community in Arkansas has had a long and productive relationship with AG & F.

I mention this because it is more difficult to appreciate the fact that our AG & F is joining the effort to kill fish-eating birds in Arkansas. For details, you can look at an article by Leslie Newell Peacock in *Arkansas Times* (August 5, 2004, page 10). She reported that AG & F personnel cooperated in attempts to destroy the Double-crested Cormorant breeding colony at Millwood Lake. "The irony that a bird native to Arkansas is being shot for nesting at a man-made lake stocked with a Florida strain of bass has not been lost on many biologists, who found the report appalling—and ridiculous," wrote Peacock. Further, at the time *Arkansas Birds* was published in 1986, we had lost all of the former breeding cormorants in Arkansas (see pages 79–81). I remember with excitement when the first cormorants were found nesting at Millwood. I have never felt comfortable about damming free-flowing streams, but I must say that when Millwood produced nesting cormorants (as well as many other birds and rare migrants), I felt this "good" had balanced the environmental "bad" of stream damage.

I find it difficult to accept a public agency funded with both game

Great Blue Heron standing on nest along Butler Creek near Beaver
Lake on March 15, 2003.

and nongame taxes undertaking to support destruction of a native
breeding bird, even if it is a now "common" one that is unpopular in
some quarters. Unfortunately, opening this door is likely to impact other
native birds, too. I wonder if that guy and his sons in Benton County
who thought they were improving their fishing by shooting GBHs will
now feel vindicated? And what about the law enforcement officer and
judge, who sided with the basic logic behind laws that protect migratory
birds?

It's all about economics, some will say. It was also "all about economics" when the first laws were passed protecting migratory birds.
It was public policy versus the economics of hard-pressed Arkansas

chicken farmers who shot all hawks species because a few hawk species caught chickens and folks in Florida who shot nesting egrets for their feathers. A century has passed; the pressing issues remain.

Peacock also mentions that AG & F has requested a new kind of permit for all of its fish hatcheries that would allow expedited killing of birds that eat fish. At the hatchery I have birded at for twenty-five-plus years (Craig, at Centerton in Benton County), I have seen how a good-sized flock of cormorants and pelicans can suddenly appear and obviously consume lots of fish being raised for release in streams and lakes. This is a direct loss. GBHs are at the hatchery all year, but are particularly numerous after the breeding season, as fledglings get their start in life. Lots of fish go down those long skinny necks. These birds add pressures to hatcheries.

Birds make headlines, but the problems in this industry seem varied: groundwater pollution, groundwater shortages, human population growth, growing stocking requests resulting from construction of new lakes and ponds, rising land prices (that inhibit expansion of the hatcheries), the need to build new and expensive hatcheries, the need to directly improve job quality for hatchery and fish farm workers, new disease strains that kill or damage fish, etc.

The hatcheries and fish farms do a lot of good for migratory birds. They make up in part for massive habitat losses caused by other activities like draining wetlands. However, I don't think it's fair to assign all fish business problems to migratory birds.

Max and Helen Parker (and others) found a healthy, vocalizing Royal Tern at a private fish farm at Lonoke in June 1986. The Parkers knew the bird would have to be thoroughly documented; it was a first, fully verified state record and a relatively new thing in the Land of Opportunity. They returned the following day, and found the bird dead, where it had been shot, like other birds, foraging at a private fish farm. The Parkers got the dead bird and delivered it to Doug James, who prepared the specimen now in the U of A collection.

The Royal Tern killing illustrates the problem of a fundamentally "open season" on birds at private fish farms, at public lakes (like Millwood), and potentially at our state hatcheries. Some of this killing could be done in a relatively "sensitive" way; that is, in a way (like integrated pest management) in which appropriate technology is carefully

American Avocet at Centerton on August 31, 2004. These large, dramatic shore-birds migrate through northwest Arkansas in small numbers in both spring and fall.

applied by qualified individuals to highly specific problem areas; that can do some long-term good, without also having widespread negative impacts undermining the rational for the original action. This could possibly work with real oversight, with care taken to protect the public resource (migratory birds). But in fact, it's unlikely there could be real oversight.

Permitted killing announces to everyone that killing of migratory birds is OK. The green light gets back quickly to folks like the people who shot up the GBH rookery in Benton County and killed the Royal Tern in Lonoke County.

I know that some of my long time friends and associates at AG & F may be discomforted by my statements here. I know that some hatchery managers and fish farmers will say I don't know what I'm talking about, and I sure don't understand their problems. I honor their knowledge and notice that they have a good point. However, I lack the faith to think that if we could kill 90% of the cormorants, herons, and pelicans, that we would fundamentally and over the long run improve the "profit" centers in the public and private fish industry.

By the way, I never felt serious ill will toward the old man and his boys who shot up the Great Blues. They were probably taught this behavior. They had seen the "Blue Cranes" eating fish and decided to put a stop to it.

2005

An Ancient Search for Ivory-bills

MAY 23

Here's some info about a search for Ivory-billed Woodpeckers (IBWs) in late 1986 in the Newport area of Jackson County. A hunter had reported seeing IBWs.

At Newport, the White and Cache Rivers are maybe ten or fifteen miles part, and a world of swampy bottomland hardwood habitat lies between them. The 2004–2005 IBW sightings have occurred approximately fifty miles south, near Brinkley. This is within the historic range: in 1885, IBWs were said to be present in "unfrequented swamps" in the Newport vicinity.

Nigel Ball and I volunteered to check it out. Nigel, from the UK, was a post-doc doing avian sleep research at University of Arkansas-Fayetteville. On December 27, Nigel and his family (including spouse Maggie, and children Hazel and Thomas), and my family (including Nancy Edelman and our daughter Ariel) arranged ourselves in the Ball's commodious car and set out across state to Newport.

At Newport we met Mr. Harold Hagar (who lived in Tuckerman, approximately eight miles north of Newport) and went with him to a bottomland hardwood forest with cypress near Diaz (north edge Newport on Highway 67). This is in the Village Creek flood plain, between the White and the Cache. Hagar stated that he saw two IBWs while hunting in this area in October 1985. The impression he made on us was a levelheaded person who knew the difference between Pileateds and IBWs.

The habitat we saw during our visit was primarily small-medium sized trees with scattered huge cypress stumps from a much earlier logging. The fact that the area had been logged since Mr. Hagar's sightings considerably dampened our spirits. From the Diaz area, we drove toward Tuckerman and saw some more bottomland hardwood habitat. It also had been logged, but not as heavily. Many large trees remained. Overall, the habitat looked better here, though Hagar had not seen IBWs at Tuckerman.

On December 28 we birded along Highway 14, southeast of Newport, in the Cache River area. Here we found some trees in the sixty- to seventy-foot range, and many, many more enormous stumps; one had a big river birch growing from inside the stump—a second-growth forest coming on! We also found a few trees in the one-hundred-foot height range. The water was frozen and the winter birding good: lots of Hermit Thrushes, creepers, Rusty Blackbirds, and numerous Hairy Woodpeckers—a bird strongly associated with mature forests. Alas for us in 1986, no IBWs.

Our search was far from thorough. We had fun mucking around in some country very different than the Ozark uplands of northwestern Arkansas. From what I've heard about the recent searches in the Brinkley area, we would probably have had to spend a whole heck of a lot more time (like a thousand times more!) than we did to do real justice to Mr. Hagar's observations. It was midwinter, and we were out with our families during the Christmas vacation.

Tail of a Snake

JUNE

Each year during the Red-cockaded Woodpecker nesting season on the Ouachita National Forest, I get to spend several weeks visiting all of the nesting groups. I take my spotting scope and binoculars and try to figure out the identity of the adult birds feeding young in the nest cavities. In essence, our whole year of work aimed at recovery of RCWs comes down to the outcomes during these few weeks of nesting.

When I was out on June 7, I heard adult RCWs calling loudly and excitedly. I assumed, correctly, they were gathered in vicinity of the nest tree. I figured this would be an easy job for me that day: all of the adults in one place. I quietly worked my way around the area and found a good place at some distance (to limit my disturbance) where I could observe and identify bands on the birds' legs. However, when I swung the spotting scope around to that point, I saw, not an RCW feeding the nestling, but rather the tail of a black rat snake poking out of the hole.

Rat snakes and I go a long ways back. I used to find them in weedy lots as a kid growing up in Fort Smith. They figured prominently in my graduate research. I had seen snakes in RCW cavities before, including one in 1992 that had three perfect lumps which, of course, were remains of three young woodpeckers banded just the week before. There is an ancient relationship between cavity nesting birds and tree climbing snakes, but at least in our time the snakes have been plentiful, and the birds—or at least these woodpeckers—rare. So while a predation event like that I witnessed on June 7 has a long natural history, it is frustrating, to say the least, when our disturbed ecosystems are unbalanced and so much rides on getting the snakes to eat something besides rare woodpeckers.

We use snake guards on RCW nest and roost trees, but as the event of June 7 shows, snakes get around or over them at times. When this happens, our whole year of work on RCW population growth is frustrated. But before we put too much of the blame on our snakes, there is more to consider.

Eastern Bluebirds investigating a potential nest cavity in Fayetteville on February 12, 2003.

In terms of recruiting young RCWs into our population, we have had four excellent years previous to this season. From 2001 through 2004, we estimate there were 176 fledglings, or slightly more than 40 per year. This compares well to the previous decade, 1990–2000, when recruitment amounted to an estimated 171 birds, or about 17 per year. This year we are going to fall below the good recruitment years. It's not just snakes, either.

Very early in the nesting season we began to notice problems—smaller clutch sizes, and rapid reduction of the broods to just one or two nestlings; in many cases, the young disappearing entirely—but with no evidence snakes were involved. The whole thing seems more likely related to weather and insect abundances. Nesting season 2005 may prove to be a year when the adults had their work cut out for them just staying alive, with little left over for rearing young birds. If this is the case, then what affected RCWs here in 2005 probably affected other cavity nesting birds as well.

Those who watch bluebird boxes may notice something. We notice these changes in nesting output of RCWs on the Ouachita NF because we watch closely—but such things typically go unnoticed for other birds.

We have been wondering if west Nile virus has affected the adults (as it has affected some other bird populations—crows, jays, etc.). Was it too hot and dry during the critical early nest period?

Former Round Prairie

JUNE

I have an 1890 Arkansas Geological Survey book that includes information on named prairies in Benton County. I've been birding some of these areas. Most are still prime grasslands, though not native grasses, and some of the best open country habitat in northwestern Arkansas. The native Tallgrass Prairie is long gone, but you can hear echoes at least in some of the birds.

One of these is the former Round Prairie, along the Arkansas-Oklahoma border in western Arkansas (look for Cherokee City on your state map). I was out there on June 5 and June 18. Most of my birding was on Floyd Moore Road. I picked this road because it is long and straight, basically connecting Highways 43 and 59. "Long and straight" in this country means it once was prairie with few obstructions. This road is directly north of the SWEPCO's Flint Creek power plant; the big stack is always visible in the south. This area is also directly north of SWEPCO's Eagle Watch Nature Trail, a comfortable place to view Bald Eagles in winter.

What I wanted to see were the open-country birds of summer: shrikes, kestrels, dickcissels, Grasshopper Sparrows, etc. I was not disappointed. Here's an abbreviated list from the two days:

American Kestrel: a single bird, and 4 together
  (presumably a family group)
Northern Bobwhite: 3 calling

Grasshopper Sparrow on security fence at Siloam Springs airport on August 3, 2008. They nest on open grasslands of our former prairies, including places like airports.

Eurasian Collared-Dove: scattered in the area

Yellow-billed Cuckoo: 6 + calling from various woodlots and fencerows

Bewick's Wren (brown; eastern form): seen in 2 spots; one a single singing bird; second was 2 birds

Loggerhead Shrike: saw birds in 5 scattered spots, including 2 family groups (one with 5 birds)

Warbling Vireo: 2

Grasshopper Sparrow: singing in one hayfield that is mostly fescue, but includes some native forbs like Baptisia

Blue Grosbeak: 4

Painted Bunting: 3 or 4

Great-tailed Grackle: 2 spots

Orchard Oriole and Baltimore Oriole: latter near Cherokee City in 4 spots

Loggerhead Shrike just out of the nest near Centerton on May 23, 2004. Shrikes were once much more common in northwest Arkansas. They have declined as their required open area habitat becomes built up through urbanization.

Overall, this area has been less obviously impacted by rapid population growth in northwest Arkansas than others. I assume this is because it is an important poultry producing country and big chicken houses means there is a need for big fields for spreading litter.

Long may this and the other former prairies of western Arkansas remain open, grassy, lightly-developed, and shrike-friendly.

Swainson's Hawks and Painted Buntings Galore

JULY

Mike Mlodinow and I made our somewhat annual trip to look for Benton County's summer Swainson's Hawks on July 2. We were not disappointed. We had GREAT looks at three. The first was just north of Maysville, at the intersection of Highway 43 and Wet Prairie Road. It perched nicely, right in front of us, in a walnut tree (I have a 99 KB image file in case anyone wants to see a genuine Arkansas Swainson's). We saw the other two together from Floyd Moore Road, east of Cherokee City. Both of these areas are former prairies.

While no longer prairies in a botanical sense, they both have extensive grasslands. Other birds of interest: we found two flocks of Horned Larks in the Maysville area: one with at least 20 birds, the other with at least 6; both were in harvested bean fields. We found Painted Buntings basically "all over the place." I figure at least 5 in the Maysville area, and at least 6 along Floyd Moore. There are nice thickets and fencerows along most of the big fields. This provides a lot of Painted habitat. Mike saw 2 Cedar Waxwings at Maysville; I was off recording mockingbird songs and didn't get up the road in time. We also found Lark Sparrow (1) and Bell's Vireo (1), plus shrikes, kestrels, and Grasshopper Sparrows singing in at least three fields.

I celebrated July 4 with a brief early morning trip to the old Norwood Prairie, located about fifteen miles west of Fayetteville, basically between Fayetteville and Siloam Springs. I found 4 Lark Sparrows, 4 Painteds, and Grasshopper Sparrows singing in one field (so that makes at least two fields in this area with Grasshopper Sparrows). I'd gone out there to record mockingbirds, but got distracted. In one recording I have Painted Bunting, Indigo Bunting, and Blue Grosbeak, all in the same regenerating field—a nice and predictable ecological songfest. When I listened to this section at home, I found that I had also recorded a Lark Sparrow.

Last evening (July 6) I made a brief (one and a half hours) tour after work. I left the office in Waldron (Scott County) at 6:00 p.m. and

Family of Scissor-tailed Flycatchers along Highway 248 in Scott County west of Waldron on June 24, 2004.

finished about 7:30. Altogether I slowly drove five or six miles of farm roads—big fields with heavy fencerows, etc. This is also former prairie: the whole area features large prairie mounds highly visible after the hale is baled. I saw 8 Painteds (7 males, 1 female) and heard (but didn't see) at least 2 others. I wasn't out specifically for Painteds, but I did feel overwhelmed by the numbers yesterday, and generally the numbers of Painteds since July 2.

All of this tends to confirm a growing feeling on my part that Painted Buntings are at least fairly common birds in the whole former prairie region in western Arkansas, at least from Scott County north to Benton County (including the Arkansas River valley). When their singing is strong—as in the last week at least—they are obviously widespread and at least relatively numerous in suitable habitat. This is farm country, with hayfields, cattle, chicken houses, and fencerows. It's big cloud country. It's Painted Bunting country.

Female Dickcissel with food for a nestling hidden in native grasses at Chesney Prairie Natural Area on August 21, 2004.

Henslow's Sparrows and Swainson's Hawk at Pea Ridge

JULY

Mike Mlodinow and I counted at least 6–7 HENSLOW'S SPARROWS at Pea Ridge National Military Park in Benton County on July 9. I also saw an adult SWAINSON'S HAWK. This trip was a follow-up to the discovery of a single Henslow's there by Mike and David Chapman during International Migratory Bird Day, May 14. Mike and David had not found them in previous years, so Henslow's there may be recent.

The birds are in an expansive, grassy field, immediately north of the visitor's center. Cost to get into the park: five dollars per car—good for visiting one week.

Henslow's Sparrow in the open fields at Wilson Springs on May 14, 2005. The presence of this rare bird during the nesting season precipitated a controversy over the future of open bottomlands along Clabber Creek in Fayetteville. Unfortunately, most nesting habitat was ultimately lost to development.

After paying our five dollars, we walked back out the front doors, around the west side of the building, crossed the tour road, hopped the split-rail fence soldier-like (well, old soldiers—maybe like those ole graybeards that used to come to reunions in the 1890s), but with binoculars rather than muskets, and marched (well, strolled?) directly out into the grassy fields. What you see out there are Civil War artillery emplacements—three or four big guns then some space, then more guns. Closest to the visitor's center are the Union lines, which face roughly northeast to the Confederate lines—more lines of big guns. The space in-between—just a few hundred yards—is a grassy field now, but was a sea of suffering humanity in March 1862.

The grass in 1862 must have been one of the common Tallgrass Prairie species (Big Bluestem, Little Bluestem, etc.). Today it's about 100% introduced Johnson grass—a strongly invasive weed that, from the looks of things July 9, works OK for Henslow's. We covered maybe half of the big field. There were probably even more Henslow's than we actually counted. One of the best things is that this is public land. Since it is the core of this bloody battlefield—called in Civil War days "the Gettysburg of the West"—it will be maintained as such in perpetuity. This is good news for a grassland species like Henslow's. However, there wasn't much of anything else in the field, birdwise—surprisingly few meadowlarks and dickcissels, for example. I suppose that may be a result of it's being a Johnson grass monoculture.

Time is certainly a trickster. My relatives of 143 years ago who served in the war (on both sides—northern Arkansas was thoroughly divided) probably saw this field where on July 9, 2005, Mike and I eagerly listened for, and enjoyed watching, a small sparrow inhabiting a big space.

Also, the wonder of all of this is that this is, as I said, public land. Emotionally, it became so because of the blood letting of 1862. It was saved from development years ago by the dedication of local history buffs. It may now play a role in protection for one of our much-declined grassland birds.

Status Designations

SEPTEMBER

Mike Mlodinow and I birded Lake Atalanta at Rogers on Sunday 9–18. Overall, a pretty slow day, and nothing truly fancy to report:

— flycatchers: Pewee, Acadian (one singing! and a second probable), *Empidonax* species, Phoebe

— vireos: White-eyed (at least 7), Yellow-throated, Blue-headed, Red-eyed

— warblers: Nashville, Parula, Black-and-white, Redstart, Yellowthroat, Wilson's (~8, still pretty numerous), Canada (2), Chat

We also had out first fall Rose-breasted Grosbeak and at Centerton, our first Savannah Sparrow.

There was a big rain up our way in the middle of the week. Mike spent the day combing Mt. Sequoyah in Fayetteville (mature upland hardwoods, mainly) and had 11 warbler species for the day. During fall, this is equivalent to a big spring fall-out.

During the drive time between Fayetteville and our Benton County birding spots, we get in lots of bird chat. Mike brought with him a tight little list of dickey birds (AKA Neotropical migrants) and their status according to the current Arkansas Audubon Society field list. It's hard to square some of the status designations (common, uncommon, rare, etc.) on the field list with what we see in the field in northwest Arkansas. Mike has carefully collected data since the 1980s, charts it all, figures frequencies, and hence has a pretty good grasp of whether or not a bird like Wilson's Warbler is really "uncommon," as stated on the field list. We see them often on our fall trips, so the bird can hardly be called "uncommon"—especially say compared to migrant Bay-breasted Warblers, which the list also notes as being "uncommon" but which we rarely see in northwest Arkansas. So who is responsible here? Well, let's start with *moi*.

One of the problems is that eastern and western Arkansas are quite different in terms of many of the ranges of these birds. Also, and I really

Killdeer incubating four eggs near Maysville on June 12, 2010.

hate to have to own up to this in such a public forum: some of the apparently rogue status designations likely date to the work I did on this field list in the mid-1980s. As far as I know, Mike is the only person in Arkansas who has actually collected enough field data in fall land-bird migration to confidently chart frequencies that can be translated into some standardized language like "common" versus "uncommon." What I did in the mid-1980s was to look at all of the card files on hand and make some intelligent (???—pretty speculative statement!)—or what I then hoped was intelligent—guesses about status. I got other folks to look at this list before Arkansas Audubon Society published it. Subsequent editions of the list have been reviewed and reviewed. Unfortunately, we do not have statewide data to make confident statements about the status of many of these birds in migration. These would be good, highly useful studies.

The Mike Mlodinow *Experience,* is the way I think about it. Bird 'til you drop, then go home and analyze what you've found out. If we had some strategically spaced "Mikes" scattered around the state, we'd have a chance to fine tune our list, which is a wonderful product, even with the above-stated caveats. They would need an interest in mathematics, which is what lies behind Mike's analysis of bird field data.

It would be useful sometime if all/most with a particular interest in this topic could assemble in a room somewhere and sort some of this out. Maybe Bay-breasts and Wilson's are of similar abundances in migration? Or is this an east-west thing? Or am I getting too old to crane my head back far enough to see Bay-breasts, or what (compared to Wilson's, which I have in my yard, nearly eye level, routinely, in migration)?

Storming the Gates of Heaven

SEPTEMBER

Mike Mlodinow and I birded Lake Atalanta in Rogers on 9/11 and Chesney Prairie Natural Area near Siloam Springs on 9/13.

At Lake Atalanta we came up with the following:

—Acadian Flycatcher, 1

—Least Flycatcher, 3 +, (and several more empids)

—vireos: White-eyed, 7; Yellow-throated, 2; Warbling, 1; Red-eyed, 2

—warblers: Parula, ~10; Magnolia, 1; Black and white, 2; Redstart, 1; Louisiana Waterthrush, 1 (possibly 2; relatively "late"; the one was a close study); Kentucky, 3 (together!); Mourning, 1 (adult male type plumage, so a different bird than last week); Wilson's, ~10 ("all over the place"); Canada, 1.

Up to today (9/14), we have had a powerful drought affecting everything here. It is no wonder, then, that some of the most interesting birding has been in the shady, moist, relatively cool Frisco Spring run with its lush vegetation, even in this drought. I suspect what we are seeing is the working of a natural reality of life in the spring region of the Springfield Plateau section of the Ozarks. Here the life processes go on, much as in

Fledgling Great Horned Owls at the University farm in Fayetteville during International Migratory Bird Day May 14, 2005.

a typical moist summer: many flowers and birds. Hummingbird numbers are still high in the abundant jewelweed patches. It adds to my sense of loss about the amount of damage being done natural springs in the mad rush to squeeze every possible dollar out of the landscape of northwest Arkansas.

A small farm pond on the drive into Chesney Prairie held 23 Great Egrets and 2 Snowy Egrets—both good records for the western Ozarks. We saw our first harrier of the season at Chesney. Most kingbirds have migrated south already, but there were 4 at Chesney. We found 3 Sedge Wrens, but they have basically stopped singing, and they were not generous with views or even *chap-chap* calls. They melt into tall, lush grasses (especially Big Bluestem in the lower parts of the prairie).

It's late in the season, but we were not surprised by finding a number of Dickcissels, Indigo Buntings, and Common Yellowthroats in the dense grasses and forbs at Chesney. I had a flock of Indigos in a head-high patch of giant ragweed, poke, goldenrod, and some Big Bluestem. It's like summer is still with us, at least in respect to these birds.

It was Northern Bobwhites—bobwhite quail—that were "storming the gates of heaven." I am using that phrase from the writings of artist Walter Inglis Anderson, of Ocean Springs, Mississippi. He was referring to a juvenile green heron that he found, wanted to paint, and that was trying to escape (he did paint it, and it is one of his masterpieces—from the book, *The Horn Island Logs of Walter Inglis Anderson*). Mike and I saw one covey of about 10 full-grown birds on Chesney proper. They stormed the gates of heaven in the usual manner—exploding at our feet, up, up, and away, and gone into Chesney's waves of grass and goldenrod. We found a second covey just south of Chesney. This was an adult male and maybe 10 half-grown chicks. They were crossing a recently harvested hayfield and heading for a dense roadside thicket. We were between them and the thicket of greenbriar, blackberry, foxtail grass, etc.—their gate to heaven. They remained on the ground until we stepped out of the car, then BOOM, all of them up and away (including the youngsters), and into heaven. Heaven seems a flexible domain, providing a supplicant's appropriate needs.

Brinkley

SEPTEMBER

I had the very good fortune to attend the fall meeting of the Arkansas Chapter of the Wildlife Society, September 15–16. It was held in Brinkley, at the Brinkley Convention Center, same as for our upcoming fall Arkansas Audubon Society meeting. The Thursday afternoon presentations got us up to speed on the multiagency, multifaceted approach underway in regards Ivory-bills. Arkansas Game & Fish Commission folks generously hosted us on a Friday morning canoe trip on Bayou de View, Dagmar Wildlife Management Area, a few miles west of Brinkley.

What an incredible place. You leave the heavily developed Delta farm country and enter a tupelo-cypress wonderland cut from the cloth of the nineteenth century. It's black water and cypress knees; for me, the presence of Ivory-billed Woodpeckers was palpable. Some of the Dagmar folks directed me for land birding to the Apple Lake area along Bayou de View, also near Brinkley. There is an easily walked elevated levee (originally built for a railroad) that provides great views of this habitat. I can't image an easier way to see a real live swamp, and—lucky for us—a chance to see/hear Ivory-bills. Oops, guess that *kent* call was just a White-breasted Nuthatch, but you never know.

Mosquitoes were a minor nuisance on the float, but the Apple Lake walk was . . . well . . . something else. This may not be such an issue at the end of October, but for this meeting I was super-duper proud that I'd brought my dear ole bug jacket (made from mosquito and no-see-'em netting) and also that the AG & F folks were generous with their supply of insect repellent. I've never tried to bird this area in late October, so I don't know what the situation vis-a-vis mosquitoes will be like then. Probably no problem, but I'm going to come prepared and will probably do this hike again.

A Birder's Fall Colors

OCTOBER

I wake up before daylight on September 14 and hear *seep* notes over-head. *Seep* then *seep seep* equals sparrows overhead, fall colors heading south. After the long, late summer drought, *seep* in the night sky prom-ises good birding ahead.

And it has been an interesting fall so far in northwestern Arkansas: big wads of mixed species sparrows and other seed eaters. There was nothing to electrify or to set off a listing stampede toward Fayetteville, but it was informative and pleasurable. (What follows is primarily from my own notes—I know in many cases my frequent birding partner Mike Mlodinow saw some of these earlier than the dates I list.)

First of the obviously migrant sparrows, Savannah Sparrow, was at the state fish hatchery at Centerton in Benton County on Sept. 18: 1–2 birds. I got my first Clay-colored Sparrow September 26 at Razorback Golf Course in Fayetteville (same day as a BIG monarch migration, for you b'fly folks). An unfortunately poor look at what was probably a "late" Lark Sparrow, a small flock of Savannahs, numerous Lincoln's Sparrows, a last small flock of Indigo Buntings (with snatches of the summer song) all at Chesney Prairie Natural Area in Benton County on October 3.

October 7 at Chesney was a real banner day for the sparrow busi-ness: first Song Sparrows, Swamp Sparrows, first junco (one of the *cismontanus* types with reddish-pink in the flanks), White-throated Sparrows, and a brownish Blue Grosbeak which tied the local "late" departure date for our area. First White-crowned Sparrows at former Norwood Prairie near Wedington west of Fayetteville, 4 birds sprinkled around in three spots, on October 8. At Hindsville in Madison County on October 15: a flock of at least 8 Vesper Sparrows, and 2 Grasshopper Sparrows (getting "late" for these summer residents).

First LeConte's: at Chesney on October 21, about the colors of the seasoned Big Bluestem grasses there.

October 11—my first local Golden-crowned Kinglet of the season plus a nice bonus of 3 brown and black tarantulas crossing a Forest Service road in Scott County.

Black Vultures cleaning up a carcass near Beaver Lake following the fall deer-hunting season.

At Hindsville on October 20, I spent a couple of hours following a mixed-species flock that included at least Clay-colored, Field, Vesper, Savannah, Grasshopper, Lincoln's, and White-crowned; Common Yellowthroat, Orange-crowned Warbler, and House Wren were in the same mix. There was a big "black warrior" (Audubon's words) western Red-tailed Hawk that at first looked, for all the world, like a standard Turkey Vulture with a nonstandard rufous tail.

After a month of birding's fall colors, I'm getting a little tired and have the start of a cold. I had some trim painting on my house that I didn't accomplish. I wanted to travel out to see my sisters, but didn't. While Mike tramps the smartweed edges at Centerton on October 22, I relax on a pond levee and stare into a blue sky, then fall asleep, flat on my back (binoculars and all) under Benton County's big fall sky. Suddenly awake, I hear Savannah *seep* notes and see a single white pelican, soaring low and slow over one of the hatchery ponds. One pelican?

Now here's Mike coming up after a long tramp of two big ponds: he's worked a small flock along a narrow brushy edge that includes Field, Savannah, Song, Lincoln's, and Swamp sparrows, plus a Marsh Wren.

Arkansas Audubon Society Meeting, Brinkley, Arkansas

OCTOBER 28–30

In response to a requested report on last weekend's Arkansas Audubon Society meeting, please accept these notes:

One thing that stands out for me: there are few opportunities to center any kind of a meeting around something as wonderful as a rediscovered "extinct" bird. Lots of people came, myself included, not because of a good chance to see THE bird, but because it was there . . . and who knows, on a given day, a birder might get really, really lucky. My evidence for good turnout despite a poor chance to see THE is as follows: 50 people with thousand-dollar bins around their necks, standing most of the day on a bridge in rural Monroe County, purely on the basis of a good rumor of a recent sighting that THE was there on the previous Monday. As far as I know, there has NEVER been such an organized field trip at an AAS meeting. Wow! I'm not sure anyone would stand around that long if one hundred dollar bills were promised to all who completed six hours on a busy bridge in eastern Arkansas.

All that, plus the unplanned musical accompaniment (a dance with "loud music" next door attended by African American youth) toward the end of Saturday night's finale—an irritation to be sure for us "quiet" birders, but also a gift, really—a reminder that the world is bigger than that part we choose to see through our bins or hear through our finely honed ears. I hope we can find ways to reach out in an inclusive way to the wider community in Brinkley and Monroe County. Our society—and the ornithological community in general everywhere—is heavily drawn from a narrow racial spectrum—not by design or because we are a bunch of racists—but because of history and its aftermath. We don't have to be victims of such history. But it is a steep challenge to overcome.

It occurred to me that all of us on that bridge—waiting for "Elvis" (code name for Ivory-billed Woodpecker)—are much like those who seek another Elvis at various places around Memphis. We have faith. We await the defining moment.

Loons

NOVEMBER

I liked Jeff Wilson's loon (s, actually—four species) webpage: www.pbase.com/ol_coot/loon_species. If any of you on the list are like me—looney, but not that good at separating the four species—this is a wonderful primer. Like being out there with Jeff. It's become a cold-weather tradition. Find those drowned rivers turned into clear water lakes. Find the birds that we can now see that were absent in the bad old days, before the rivers became reservoirs. Many of the images are like what you'd get on a great day at a place with the four species—down and dirty through the scope—with waves and Charles Mills quality "heat shimmers"—and that odd way that much-longed-for birds (viewed at great distance) rarely cooperate for the perfect profile—and with the Ol' Coot himself whispering in your ear about the location of the high point on the back of that loon, and how that high point isn't in the center of the back on that other loon. I started at Jeff's first loon, then slowly worked my way through the four species, clicking "next," and "next" and reading his Roger Tory Peterson style "key marks" play-by-play. Within four images the warm world of my office had segued to cold wind tearing through my jacket, numb fingers, and furious focusing my spotting scope. It's in Tennessee, but it's the same in Arkansas (on a VERY lucky day) and at Tenkiller in eastern Oklahoma.

I have found that seeking and seeing loons is a season high point for me as a birder. I mourn summer's passing, look forward to loon's arrival. Or I should write, loons' arrival. We see loons on Beaver Lake in northwest Arkansas, but usually just a few. Tenkiller Lake in eastern Oklahoma, seventy miles west of Fayetteville, is a different matter. All four species have been seen there in the last couple of years. I've made the hajj over there several times in the past two years. This past weekend we saw 50 or so Common Loons from the Strayhorn area, plus two Pacific Loons, but not the other two loon species. I like Jeff's description of the Pacific as "cobra head." I noticed the distinct look, but hadn't gotten that far with a descriptor.

Invitation to Fayetteville CBC 2005

NOVEMBER

Please join us on the historic and formerly well-organized Fayetteville CBC Sunday December 18, 2005. The many benefits (?) include:

1. An opportunity to rise at 4 a.m. for owling, if you wish

2. A chance to dodge any one of the hundreds of construction projects creating new "profit-centers" within the count circle

3. Fellowship with "The Best and the Birdiest" in the Fayetteville area

4. A chance to learn technical details for separating Lesser and Great Scaup as hopefully viewed on a sweet-smelling sewer pond

5. Wild romps through blackberry thickets in pursuit of Harris's Sparrows

6. Bald Eagles soaring over a Wal-Mart super center, oblivious to constantly falling prices

7. Golf Course Birding, Introductory Course 1001 (forget your clubs; bring the nokies)

8. An investment of $5, rain or shine, heat or cold. Where can you find a comparable deal for a full day's "entertainment"?

9. The coveted opportunity to defend any UNUSUAL sightings before a famously skeptical post-count confab at the home of Doug James and Elizabeth Adam. An image will help; written docs are a must. Speakers are requested to lick pizza sauce from their fingers BEFORE interrupting.

10. Please no hoot-owling out in the yard.

Western Meadowlark

DECEMBER 20, FAYETTEVILLE CBC

When it's all said and done, including count week birds, Fayetteville will come close to its own "Holy Grail," 100 species. It looks like 98 now (94 + 4 for the count week), but count week isn't over. We had lots of folks and lots of fun. The brilliant male Summer Tanager (now affectionately known as "Tannie") made an appearance at Bob and Sara Caulk's Mt. Sequoyah suet feeder, as hoped. No ice, no snow, no wind.

I'd say my biggest personal challenge for the day was finding a Western Meadowlark. The University Experimental Farm in Fayetteville is home to many wintering meadowlarks, but it has been my experience that it is a rare midwinter day when there is much singing, and Western *chups* are rarely heard. Doug James says he used to get them by spotting meadowlarks, then slowly . . . slowly . . . creeping up on them, always pausing before they fly, then creeping some more, until one bird finally gives it up and *chups*. This was years before Sibley and years before hotshot birders with super scopes picked them out by malar stripe alone.

In a manner of speaking, I have inherited the CBC-day farm and have tried Doug's technique, occasionally with success. This year I decided to go high tech and try playback. I deployed all of my finest technology on a dry run at the farm the day before the count. I did get a Western interested or perhaps I should say puzzled? I mean, just what are those strange sounds of June in Colorado doing here in Arkansas in winter???

On count day I eagerly sought out the meadowlark flocks, liberally deployed my playback, and got zapped again and again. Things were looking bad for our CBC in terms of that bird. How could a flock of 40 meadowlarks not have a single Western at least *chup* back? But there I go again with my human hubris. The reality is, how could a human think any self-respecting meadowlark would pay attention to a Colorado June in a mid-December Arkansas field? But then, it happened.

There was a huge old post oak out in an open field, with its branches filled with maybe 30 meadowlarks—all yellow against the gray of the day. I fired up the MP3 player. The cows looked strangely at us, who had no hay for them. And one Western Meadowlark sang a few—a very few—notes for us. That song from the upper boughs of an old post oak was manna from Heaven. I bent down and kissed the ground, no doubt an embarrassment to my party, especially considering it's a pasture with lots of . . . well you know . . . Not really, but I secretly wanted to.

This will doubtless sound pretty silly, especially to all who have their Western Meadowlarks all lined up and ready to be counted, and especially to anyone out West . . . where *chups* don't count for much . . . where the chase, I assume, involves Easterns and those buzzy *zapps*.

2006

Dardenelle

FEBRUARY

Kenny and LaDonna Nichols squired a group of us Fayetteville-area birders around Dardenelle Lake on Saturday February 4. Our group included Mike Mlodinow, plus Mary Bess and Paige Mulhollan. We got wonderful views of one Black and one White-winged Scoter. Besides that, we saw all of the Ruddy Ducks and Lesser Scaups the heart could desire, and views of male Canvasbacks in perfect sunlight. The north wind made the water a little choppy, made us clutch those scopes tightly, but the views from the Nichol's place were superb. That cloud of scaup rising as a boat approached was a sight of wild nature rare and wonderful.

Kenny and LaDonna teamed up in spotting the scoters for us in that choppy water. I am taking not a thing from Kenny in awarding my personal best prize to LaDonna for spotting, holding down her scope, and occasionally also holding her dog, all at the same time. In case anyone doubts, I collected images.

These wonderful days of bird chasing crank up my ambiguities. It's a two-hour drive from Fayetteville to Dardenelle. I think it's safe to say the four us in the car Saturday are concerned about greenhouse gas emissions and energy use, think Americans are addicted to their cars, and would offer the opinion that President Bush hasn't quite figured it out. Boy, is that finger ever pointing at us. Then there is the lake.

I came of age in the 1960s alternative culture and honestly, never quite grew out of it. Favorite slogan from then: "No nukes is good nukes." Dardenelle provides cooling water for the nuclear plant. While watching scoters, we could see the steam billowing from the big cooling

Expert birder Mike Mlodinow studying waterfowl through his spotting scope at Lake Fayetteville during a Northwest Arkansas Audubon Society field trip on November 15, 2009. Mike has been the most active field observer in the region for many years.

tower. I assume the elevated water temperatures associated with cooling the plant foster suitable environmental conditions and the forage base for all of those thousands upon thousands of diving ducks, not to mention white pelicans, gulls (including the California Gull), a huge flock of Snow Geese, cormorants, etc. So here I am in 2006, with my big scope, scanning diving ducks in the nuke lake.

I am grateful for friends and birders who share their treasures. I am also grateful to have reached the life stage where the many facets constituting most ambiguities are easily seen if uneasily entertained.

Dunlin and Time

FEBRUARY

This report involves Benton County in EXTREME northwestern Arkansas. I spent our one winter day this winter with Mike Mlodinow, plus Paige and Mary Bess Mulhollan, scouring the Maysville area, with a quick stop at the Eagle Watch Nature Trail just west of Gentry. The temp hovered around just below thirty all day. We had snow flurries, varying from a little to a lot. At one point, it was a thirty MPH cold wind from the west, with heavy flurries blowing straight into our eyes as we tried to look west at a field with potential for longspurs, Horned Larks, etc. It doesn't take long under such conditions to choose inside the car, even if you can't hear anything but springs in the seats, breathing, and, well, the joyful crackling of snacks.

As we drove out from Decatur we saw a knot of Bald Eagles behind some chicken houses. Eventually, we could see approx. 25 in a couple of trees, plus others lower down and mainly out of our view. We saw eagles all day, with a conservative tally of 40 and the actual number likely higher.

During one break in the wind we did hear and see a few Western Meadowlarks among many more Easterns. We found only scattered Horned Larks (5 for the day), with no large flocks. We found one flock of at least 21 American Pipits in a plowed field recently fertilized, with that and snow flurries blowing straight in at us. You think you must really love birding at such moments. You appreciate the fact that if the land continues to be productive for farming, it might remain open rather than being condemned to death by subdivision. What I'm saying here is that the smell is powerful, and I'm pleased the landowners are still farming.

There were no Lapland Longspurs for the day. Our latest local record is February 9, so the lack of them is not so surprising on February 11. Without the wind, we would have had a better chance of at least hearing them, and then perhaps finding a migrating flock. There were flocks of Savannah Sparrows all over the place. White-crowned Sparrows were plentiful, and we found a few Harris's Sparrows mixed in among them.

American Tree Sparrows near Maysville January 9, 2010. Flocks usually arrive here when ice and snow forces them south.

Most surprising for us for the day, a LINCOLN'S SPARROW, right in "downtown" Maysville, seen at very close range. We find few of them in midwinter in our part of the state, and you just don't get those kind of looks: the bird flew within 10 feet of the car, and perched out in front of god and everybody, so we could thoroughly enjoy its presence (and for me, to confirm the fine breast streaks and buffiness) in the warmth of the Mulhollan car.

We found 3 harriers in the Maysville area. I know this will make no impression whatsoever on birders in eastern Arkansas, where, for example, Dick Baxter recently had dozens in view at once as they went to roost. The 3 on February 11 is a winter "peak" for us, and each of them was completely enjoyed.

Among many "regular" Red-tailed Hawks were 2 Harlan's and 2 of the *calurus* variety—looks like a Turkey Vulture (silvery primaries and secondaries and black otherwise) with a reddish tail.

The Dunlin was on a big mudflat along SWEPCO Lake at the Eagle Watch Nature Trail. SWEPCO Lake is comparatively warm because it

White-crowned Sparrow near Vaughn in Benton County on March 6, 2010.
Singing flocks enliven many winter days here.

is used to cool the electrical generating plant. We had a Dunlin in the same area on December 31, 2005. If you look at the Christmas Bird Count Data for North America (I used the ten-year automated map feature), you can see that the winter range is overwhelmingly coastal, but with a few spots inland, including a few north of Arkansas. It is still unusual and noteworthy, and was a nice place for us to end a long and fruitful day.

It was snowing pretty hard at that point, with we birders trying to get good Dunlin looks, clouds coming up from the lake, snow falling and blowing, shorebirds probing for invertebrates in the mud.

One other note: Paige Mulhollan was my history professor and honors project advisor when I was an undergrad at U of A-Fayetteville in the late 1960s. In addition, Paige and Mary Bess have a talented son, Kelly. With his partner Donna Stjerna, they have performed as Still on the Hill and are among Fayetteville's finest musicians and producers. Kelly and Donna also teach each summer in the Halberg Ecology Camp. I listen to their CDs and have enjoyed them many evenings in clubs and coffee houses around town. If anyone had told me in 1968 that Dr. Mulhollan and I (not to mention Mary Bess) would be birding together in 2006, I would certainly have considered the possibility that they had inhaled a little too much of what was much in the air around campus that year—not to mention that a Mulhollan son and partner would be powerful, creative musical forces.

Well, here we are.

Three Mississippi Kites Soaring

AUGUST

Mike Mlodinow birded Lake Atalanta at Rogers in Benton County on Saturday, August 19. We were out to see what the migration held, and eventually identified 9 warbler species—a good fall day in the mountain forests of western Arkansas: Northern Parula, Yellow, Cerulean, Black-and-white, Prothonotary, Northern Waterthrush, Louisiana Waterthrush, Kentucky, and Mourning. We rarely find Ceruleans away from the known breeding areas, so one seen (and possibly another singing [!]) at Lake Atalanta is a treat—also a pain in the neck (treetops=warbler neck). The Mourning Warbler was an "early arrival" for the western Arkansas Ozarks; our previous early bird was August 24. We also had 2 or 3 Upland Sandpipers fly over, calling, and providing us with good looks.

I'd say we had the most fun with the two waterthrush species. Louisianas nest in our area and Northerns are fairly common migrants. We don't often find them, however, in the same place. Sure, it's always wet, but all dampness is not created equal for these birds. Birders with a few years under their belts know to look at the eye-stripe shape and color, carefully examine the throat area, and finally to note the density of the belly/flank streaking. Finally—and I say this with a bit of hesitation—consider the difference in call notes.

Mike and I were just at the head of the Frisco Spring trail when we each heard, then each noted, a waterthrush at the little bridge near the picnic pavilion. Mike sang out, "Northern Waterthrush" as I was still getting in focus. But what I saw didn't look like Northern: the eye stripe was white and broad in the rear, and when it turned, I could see clearly a plain, unstreaked throat. In short, it sure didn't look like a Northern. But I hesitated, because Mike is a genuine expert on the eastern *Parulidae*. As a friend and birding partner of his for twenty-five years, I know darn well that while I'm watching TV or mowing the grass, Mike is studying Jon Dunn and Kimball Garrett's *Peterson Field Guide Warblers*.

"Well Mike," I hesitate, "look at that eye stripe—good contrast with the flanks and it's WHITE." Mike is silent. "The THROAT! It's unmarked." Finally Mike says, "Where are you looking?" I assume we're looking at the same bird.

In just a small spot there at the bridge are at least two water thrushes. Mike sees my bird, at last, and confirms. That sends me looking. Now I have his Northern, and Mike has my Louisiana. But how many of each? Now come the *chink* notes. Who's doing that?

Off and on during the day I'm scanning the sky for Mississippi Kites, which are now migrating, but are rare in our part of the state. All of the high-flying birds look like kites to me, at least until a good look with the bins shows them to be swifts. Etc. Etc. When I get home I have a message from my neighbor, Kelly Mulhollan. He and Donna Stjerna (these are the same folks from the Halberg camp—musicians and birders) have been seeing a Mississippi Kite from their house for the past two days! Of course, I immediately run out in the yard and see swifts, but no kite. But my luck is about the change.

On Sunday evening, August 20, a friend is over for supper. My plan is to lounge inside, under the comforting benevolence of the AC, but she thinks it's cool enough for the front porch, so out we go. Immediately, I hear an *Empidonax* call that I think is a Least—"Come on, let's look at it. Don't need bins." I see the bird up in a cottonwood —and while looking up—3 hawks. Not just hawks, but kites! I race in for binoculars: 3 Mississippi Kites soaring over the neighborhood.

Woolsey Wet Prairie

DECEMBER 11

Amy Edie and I went out to the Woolsey Wet Prairie at Fayetteville on Sunday December 10, 2006. We flushed a Short-eared Owl from tall grass among the big prairie mounds that dot the place. It's a rare bird in northwest Arkansas. Besides this owl, we saw a Loggerhead Shrike, a flock of American Pipits, Savannah Sparrows, etc. The owl perched on a low limb and was swooped off the limb by a Northern Harrier. (We also had Sedge Wrens there on November 19.)

"Woolsey Wet Prairie" is a working name for a wetlands mitigation project in association with Fayetteville's new wastewater treatment plant. Woolsey is part of former lowland Tallgrass Prairie, once widespread in the prairie region of NW AR, including Fayetteville. The Ozarks, of course, are justifiably famous for scenic upland forests, but seasonally wet former prairie is our region's most endangered habitat, overall with our rarest birds. Loss of this habitat has heavily impacted many bird species. We lost a breeding location for Willow Flycatcher, for example, near the Bentonville airport. We have all but lost our breeding Bell's Vireos, once common here.

Amy and I ran into Joe Woolbright, of Ozark Ecological Restoration, Inc., at Woolsey. Joe is serving as a consultant to the contractor responsible for the project. The last Short-eared Owl I saw in NW AR was at Chesney Prairie Natural Area at Siloam Springs where Joe is doing restoration and management. Outside of Joe's work with prairies and former prairies, I am aware of only a few individuals and no institutions or conservation groups with abiding interest in protecting this increasingly rare habitat in the Ozarks region of NW AR. It's like we can't see the forest for the trees, or more precisely, the rare native grassland habitats for the forest.

On the previous day, Mike Mlodinow and I were scouting for the Fayetteville CBC and hit the former Wilson Springs area—which, like Woolsey, features a lowland former prairie. We lost the fight with the City of Fayetteville to protect two hundred plus acres of Wilson Springs (and its breeding-season Henslow's Sparrows), but it looks like about

Canada Goose with chicks at Woolsey Wet Prairie in Fayetteville on April 7, 2009.

one hundred or so acres will remain, with much of it buffer land adjacent Clabber Creek, plus a few other riparian strips and a few acres of native grasslands. Among other birds, we found 2 or 3 Sedge Wrens—a "good" bird for winter at Fayetteville and a treasure for our CBC. At least it will not all be developed. There will be birding opportunities adjacent the heavy development along I-540.

It's agonizing to see fields that supported Henslow's, American Bitterns, Soras, Short-eared Owls, etc. being turned into a Sam's Club, an eight-thousand-square-foot liquor store, upscale housing, etc. Locating and protecting significant parcels of lowland former seasonally wet prairie in the Ozarks could be an important and rewarding challenge for the conservation community in Arkansas. It is my hope that construction of the wastewater treatment (AKA, sewage) plant will retard housing and commercial development around Woolsey, keeping the area in big open fields, as it is today, and giving a better chance for the kind of birds we saw Sunday.

Every acre we lose pushes a group of bird species closer to the time when they become listed as threatened or endangered, with huge long-term management costs for society. That's why protecting it and managing it early benefits all of society, not just the birding community.

Oh yeah, I forgot to mention that the new streets covering former prairie fields at Wilson Springs have bird names. Isn't that clever?

Bald Eagles in Winter in Benton County

DECEMBER 28

At mid-winter (best time: January) you can see many Bald Eagles in Benton County right along the highways—along 102, between Decatur and Maysville, or along 72, between Gravette and Maysville. I saw 25–40 with no effort on Christmas Day during birding around Maysville—overhead, perched in trees, standing in fields. They were numerous on Christmas Eve in and around Chesney Prairie Natural Area near Siloam Springs, also elsewhere in Benton County. All of the heavy poultry producing areas in Benton County (and generally in northwest Arkansas with heavy poultry concentrations) are attractive to Bald Eagles.

Golden Eagles are an **EXTREME** rarity in this area. Don't expect Goldens, but every age class and plumage condition of Balds is present.

The big midwinter roost is near Gravette. Doug James and his students have studied several Bald Eagle roosts in Benton County since the late 1970s, more recently near Gravette. The Arkansas Audubon Society Trust has provided funding to assist these students in their studies.

If you are interested in the roost, a good time to see a mass of birds is at dawn, as they leave. You can view them from the area of the Spavinaw Creek bridge on Highway 59, between Decatur and Gravette (find a safe place off the bridge). You can also get good views from the heights along Mt. Olive Road, also between Decatur and Gravette. Go west a short distance on Mt. Olive after turning off 59, keeping your view to the north (towards Spavinaw). Birds leaving the roost will fly up from the bottoms heading south (right overhead). I have not visited this

Bald Eagle near Chesney Prairie Natural Area on February 7, 2009. Northwest Arkansas is a great place to find these eagles in the middle of winter, and there are always at least a few on the former prairie lands of Benton County.

area in the afternoon or dusk, when I assume birds would be streaming in as well.

There is also an interesting place to see Bald Eagles near Gentry— the Eagle Watch Nature Trail west of Gentry (more information on this below). Eagles do not night roost there with regularity, but during the peak times (midwinter) they are almost always there during the day.

I would encourage everyone with an interest in this topic to remember that eagles are federally listed as threatened; don't harass the birds and stay out of the roost! The roost is on private rather than public property and the property owners are very protective of "their" birds.

Here are some details about the Eagle Watch Nature Trail in case you head up that way:

Notice Highway 59 on your Arkansas highway map. Gentry is at the intersection of 59 and Highway 12. From this intersection, travel west on 12 for approximately two miles. The Eagle Watch Nature Trail is approx. one mile west of the city limits on the south side of the highway. Look for the parking lot on the highway's south side, immediately east of the highway bridge spanning Little Flint Creek. There is an information sign in the parking area.

The approx. 1,500 acres of EWNT are part the five-hundred-acre SWEPCO Lake, constructed to provide cooling water for the coal-fired plant generating electricity for northwest Arkansas. During winter, temperatures in the lake average in the low seventies. This warm water is presumably the source of some interesting bird records.

The parking lot is the starting point for a trail that is 0.5 miles long (1 mile round trip). The trail is well marked, generally level, and easily walked because of a thick bed of mulch. The first 0.3 miles include open fields and the Little Flint Creek bottoms. There is a farm to the east, and a forested ridge to the west. The final 0.2 miles includes an optional steeper path into typical Ozark woodland. The trail ends at an attractive pavilion that provides tables, an appealing overlook of part of the lake and forested ridges, and information about the flora and fauna of EWNT.

Many visitors want to see Bald Eagles, which are present during winter. The best time to see them is probably from late November through early March. The eagles perch on snags out in the lake and in trees along the lake's edge. Also look for them soaring overhead anywhere along the trail. It's possible to visit EWNT and miss them. If that happens, try the lake's boat ramp: from Gentry, travel west on 12 to Cripps Road, turn south, travel about two miles to the boat ramp and parking area (this turn is about one mile west of EWNT).

2007

Battle for the Buffalo

JANUARY 17

I took advantage of the holidays and winter weather for birding and reading. On my list was Neil Compton's *The Battle for the Buffalo River* (University of Arkansas Press, 1992). This is an amazing book. Birders and their concern for the environment played an important role in saving the Buffalo from at least two planned dams and the local congressman aggressively pushing them.

Here are a few pertinent factoids: our own Arkansas Audubon Society (**AAS**) was the first organized statewide group to take a forthright stand against dams on the Buffalo River. Doug James, Fran James, William Shepherd, Hank and Luvois Shugart, and others—early members or **AAS** founders—stood up in the early 1960s and fought for a free-flowing river, fought against the odds when it seemed highly likely the Buffalo would drown as had most mountain rivers in the Ozarks.

Today's living, breathing habitat for Neotropical migrants, numerous rare plants, and places for people in a natural environment is owed to what others (including those who would form the Ozark Society) freely gave. Otherwise, it would have all been buried under powerboats, marinas, and exotic fish.

Doug James was a critical player in this. His role is prominently displayed in the book. He went to the meetings, organized the students, used his professional skills. He and Fran used the occasion of the 1969 American Ornithologists' Union meeting at Fayetteville to get the AOU—and Roger Tory Peterson—over to the Buffalo. There is a fine picture of Peterson, Fran James, and Charles Johnston at Tony Bend on the Buffalo. It was before there was a park, when dams loomed over waterthrush habitat.

Here's something from Neil's Compton's introduction. I find it inspirational, as relevant now as during the battle:

> The struggle to save the Buffalo River in the Arkansas Ozarks brought to the fore manifestations of a worldwide plague generated by the hand and mind of man. If we in our great wisdom cannot develop insight enough to control that affliction, we might well become the principal agents in the ruination of our only possible home in the universe.
>
> It is not likely that we shall ever find sustenance on any celestial body beyond the earth. Some may provide temporary abode, but none other than the earth can harbor us on into the future. And here we have only a hairline two-dimensional surface upon which to place our feet . . . Where the earth's gaseous envelope meets dry land is our natural domain, and today we stand dominant upon it. We now exercise power to change and mutilate it in ways undreamed of a generation ago. With that power we now course the skies like angels and live like gods on terra firma. If at last we have become gods, it is now past time to extend to the earth and all of its creatures the compassion and understanding that we have hitherto assigned to the gods.

In Praise of Burrowing Crawfish, *Procambarus liberorum*

MARCH 14

I know this is going to sound pretty weird, but terrestrial crawfish are about the best ally grassland birds have in northwestern Arkansas. Low wet fields that support communities of Ozark Burrowing Crawfish are typically those in the best ecological condition—specifically because they are so wet, so low, that they have usually not been plowed and developed to death. Degraded ecologically—yes. But this is the place for Sedge Wrens, Le Conte's Sparrow, Soras in migration, Northern Harriers looking for a quick rat. Looking for a wintering Short-eared Owl? That's the habitat here. It's what's left of Bell's Vireo summer habitat in our neck of the Ozarks. This is where I go to find these birds in the Fayetteville area.

In short, when I see the characteristic mud chimneys of these terrestrial crawfish, I know I'm in good bird country. If there are remnant prairie mounds between the saucer-like depressions with chimneys, it's even better. It's where we have found nesting-season Henslow's Sparrows.

Crawfish chimneys plus prairie mounds plus scattered small wetlands with sedges equals a great place for bird diversity in our part of the state. These are a special kind of wetlands associated with the former Tallgrass Prairies. I call them "seasonal wetlands"—they are very wet at times of the year with much rainfall, but dry in others. Ecologically, they have characteristic plants and animals of both wet and dry ground.

They are not much like the perennial wetlands or marshes of southern and eastern Arkansas or those associated with the valley of the Arkansas River. They have no legal protection, really. A two-hundred-acre lowland field covered with crawfish chimneys, prairie mounds, and all kinds of bottomland native plants may not have more than a couple of acres of perennial shallow wetlands that looks "marshy." Only the perennial shallows have some legal protection as "wetland." The rest is fair game for what's called "improvement"—draining, filling, building, paving. Of course, the general view is that such land is a boggy wasteland of no value until commercially developed. This attitude seems

Le Conte's Sparrow at Woolsey Wet Prairie in Fayetteville on October 10, 2008. These jewel-like small birds can be hard to see in winter vegetation.

as endemic to our human species as terrestrial crawfish are to seasonal wetlands.

If terrestrial crawfish survive flood and drought in these clay-rich soils, the same soils and underlying water table can absorb a whole lot of rain, hold it for a while, and release it slowly. Some of this flow is expressed as springs, which are numerous in the Fayetteville area and a source of civic pride. Water that is held in such habitat also helps remove pollution and assorted impurities. Slow release reduces the danger of downstream flash flooding. All of these are economic realities—the value to birds and wildlife in general, the value of springs for personal renewal, and pure water and flood control in growing cities.

As a society, we can readily state the current price of a gallon of unleaded gas, but what is the ecological value of an acre of seasonal wetland in terms of endemic terrestrial crawfish, migrating Soras, and clean water? We will know how much when, month after month, we pay higher water bills. We will know when for flood damage we pay in lives and higher taxes. We will pay in social dysfunction when we trade diverse grasslands for overbuilt cities.

If you come to Fayetteville (as I hope many of you will do for the spring meeting of Arkansas Audubon Society April 27–29, 2007), you will probably get to see how really poor we are getting in what's called the wealthiest part of Arkansas. You'll get to see how we value "big box" retail outlets and "looks pretty much all the same" housing over our rapidly dwindling stock of seasonal wetlands and burrowing crawfish.

I-540 in the vicinity of the U of A campus and Northwest Arkansas Mall anchors parts of what's left of our once expansive headwaters of Clabber Creek. There were originally thousands of acres of seasonal wetlands here; a few hundred remain. You can imagine the impacts on the many bird species dependent upon such habitat.

I laughed aloud recently when a developer planning to convert about one hundred acres of seasonal wetlands made quite a pitch about saving a couple of trees out in the middle of wetland fields to a bunch of us self-appointed guardians of truth and environment. He was shocked when I said I didn't care about them and they shouldn't be there anyway, and then in my next breath added, "Hey, look at this great crawfish chimney!" I think it's hard for tree lovers (myself included) to switch gears and recognize that our old grasslands and their crawfish also need the love.

If you come to the AAS meeting, I will try and get out with anyone interested in this subject. I don't know if it will be the BEST place for birding in late April, but it's always interesting. Thanks for listening.

Barred Owl adult roosting in mature eastern red cedar at Lake Fayetteville. These large owls thrive where there are extensive blocks of mature trees.

About Trust

MAY 3

I have serious trust issues about plans to kill Barred Owls to help Spotted Owls in the west. This doesn't mean I am necessarily opposed. It's more like I'm out there, waiting to find out what's really going on:

> The recovery plan envisions removing 12 to 32 barred owls in each of 18 areas, first by luring them with recorded calls and an owl decoy, then by shooting them at close range. (news report)

I think this will be a stormy debate, as it should be. Perhaps removal could work, and serious, well-meaning biologists are involved in this proposal. I can see that the science involved may be on the side of reducing Barred Owls, which I agree are not rare. But the trust problem for me is derived from the internal workings of some folks charged with solving such problems and what motivates their proposed solutions. For example, one scenario is that this alternative is being chosen because someone in an involved agency is trying to inappropriately protect private interests operating on public land. Let me say clearly, I do not know that this is the case (proposed killing of Barred Owls instead of protecting additional habitat).

We need to be able to trust officials involved in such things. If we cannot trust them, it is hard to support such plans, even if it might help a rare species.

I have professional experience that makes my head spin in these situations. I have been working on Red-cockaded Woodpecker recovery on the Ouachita National Forest in Arkansas for the past fifteen years. Early on, we discovered that southern flying squirrels were a common and even abundant rodent. They used many cavities needed for RCW recovery. We found that removing squirrels helped move us toward our RCW recovery goals. In the course of capturing and relocating flying squirrels, we accidentally kill some every year. (Our captures as well as the deaths are reported each year to Arkansas Game & Fish as part of the permit allowing us to handle the squirrels.) There is a long, and complicated, biological reason why RCWs became so rare and squirrels became so abundant in the Ouachitas—another issue, for another time.

I am sure that many folks on the list would not be happy that we "disfavor" flying squirrels even though it is for what I consider a defensible cause—trying to recover RCWs. Even with our efforts, the other 85–90% of the 1.8 million acres of the Ouachita NF provides LOTS of squirrel habitat with no well-meaning biologists like me (and others) hauling them away. So in that respect it may be like the owl situation. If the public trusts us, and our intentions, we hope we will continue to be supported, even by those who appreciate RCWs AND flying squirrels.

Barred Owls are magnificent creatures. Supporting killing them on public lands with public money requires a lot of trust. We need to know that the motives are driven by biology, not politics. I do not know this at this point.

Trust is the basic issued raised in the article in part pasted below. It's really hard to keep the public supporting public officials charged with managing public resources when trust is undermined by personal incompetence or politically-motivated decisions unsupported by objective biological field work. This is hard stuff and rarely does it lend itself to black-and-white clarity.

> Interior Department official resigns (Julie Cart, *LA Times* Staff Writer May 2, 2007): "An Interior Department official who was recently rebuked for altering scientific conclusions to reduce protections for endangered species and providing internal documents to lobbyists resigned Monday, officials said. Julie A. MacDonald, a deputy assistant secretary who oversaw the Fish and Wildlife Service's endangered species program, also faced conflict-of-interest questions in a report issued by the Interior Department's inspector general in March. MacDonald's departure came a week before a scheduled congressional oversight hearing to investigate whether Bush administration officials have ignored scientific findings in their decisions on endangered species . . . In many instances, MacDonald's changes caused scientists to request that their names be removed from documents. The inspector general calculated that in the last six years, 75% of the endangered species reports from the Fish and Wildlife Service's Western offices did not have standard signoffs by scientific staff members."

This kind of stuff is really hard on trust.

The Twins, from the Traffic

JUNE 26

On a western horizon, twenty miles distant from Fayetteville, I see Wedington Ridge, in the Ozark National Forest. Sandstone beds have eroded away. What remains are South Twin and North Twin, flat-topped remnants of the ancient Ozarks, standing out mountain-like. I see the twins during a walk around Mt. Sequoyah, near my home, and make a leisurely pause to take in the grand landscape.

Later, I catch the twins again at a red light on North Street. I'm on my way to Wal-Mart. Traffic inches through heat shimmers: there's the red light, the turning light, and somebody on a cell phone; like me, they seem lost. In my case, the high place on North Street again reveals that western landscape. As I idle in line, the twins rise magic carpetlike.

I see and hear Scarlet Tanagers that nest in hardwood forests on distant, ancient twins. It's a good place in spring to seek out the first Black-and-white Warblers. There will be Whip-poor-wills and soon, Chuck-will's-widows. Emotionally, I'm far from Fayetteville's traffic noise and summer heat.

In mid-March I'm on a hike with Amy Edie and her friendly little dog, Hattie. That whole vast, hard sandstone ridge is screaming life in the massive flowering of serviceberry trees. We walk the trail through a jigsaw puzzle of sandstone slump blocks. Fresh tiger swallowtails dart among dense thickets of white serviceberry flowers. Near the top of South Twin, we find an adult Black Vulture that hisses at us from a low limb above a shallow grotto. In relative darkness inside there are two big bluish eggs.

Now the light has changed and traffic begins to move again on North Street. Driving on—we must! (?)—I lose the high spot with its magic twins.

Amy Edie on South Twin in the Ozark National Forest at Wedington on March 20, 2007. We explored an area where Black Vultures nest. We also made a trip out to the Pacific Northwest to see my daughter Ariel and some interesting birds there, including Marbled Murrelets.

Red-cockaded Woodpeckers and Marbled Murrelets

JULY 3

Nesting season 2007 for endangered Red-cockaded Woodpeckers is now over on the Ouachita National Forest in western Arkansas. The woodpeckers have had a good year and as a result, those who view endangered species recovery as an important societal goal have also had a good year. It appears the woodpeckers fledged 66 young'ns, which nicely exceeds our previous high of 49. All of us working on the woodpecker project agree that the effort is moving in the right direction. It's a very big team effort.

Ariel Kate Neal during a field trip to Mt. Rainier National Park in 2007. We were on our way up to the Paradise visitor's center and saw Stellar's Jay and Clark's Nutcracker before we even got the car parked!

First it starts with the birds themselves, then includes our Forest Service (and a few citizen volunteers) team on the Ouachita NF, and also includes all of you, who support the concept of public lands where an ideal like recovering a rare bird is a possibility because $$$ is only one part of the bottom line. That's your decision given voice through the Endangered Species Act and support for the concept of public lands. Thanks to all of you. Nesting was excellent along Buffalo Road, which is where many of you have come to view the woodpeckers.

So, Marbled Murrelets, where do they fit in? My friend Amy Edie has been encouraging me to make a trip out to the Pacific Northwest to see my daughter Ariel. I'm a reluctant traveler and the distance, time, and cost involved makes me uncomfortable. Airports and airline schedules also make me uncomfortable. But, with Amy's help and experience in travel, we soon had a plan for a trip to see Ariel in Olympia, Washington. I'm not reluctant about birding, so the plans included a trip to Neah Bay and Cape Flattery (both in northwest Washington) to see Marbled Murrelets and other seagoing birds (like Tufted Puffins) in the Pacific Northwest. We saw them from Tongue Point and on a three hour boat trip out of Neah Bay aboard the "Puffin," with an outstanding guide, Steve Boothe. The birding was fine and we also had brief looks at grey whales. Neah Bay is on the Makah Indian reservation. I also made it to the Makah museum where the close association of the Makah and the coastal environmental is well displayed. It provided a lot of food for thought for an environmentalist who is still trying to understand the balance between our modern world and the old natural world in which we must live. I felt like I had been in a graduate seminar with excellent instruction from Boothe, seabirds, and the Makah.

These murrelets are listed as a threatened species: threatened by widespread reduction of the old growth forest where they nest along the Pacific coast, and threatened by repeated oil spills at sea, where they forage. Murrelets share with our woodpeckers the common need for public lands management to include them as well as us. They also share the need for us to be aware that our everyday actions have direct impacts far away. Our big homes use a lot of wood, which fuels pressures on our forests. I used a lot of oil and gas getting out to the Pacific Northwest, and much of it probably came from tankers like those which periodically spill and kill murrelets along our coasts. So, like support for good public lands management, support for reasonable environmental standards and personal responsibility in this area can have positive impacts on the future of the murrelets, just as it can on RCWs in Arkansas.

It's kind of a package deal and it doesn't make a lot of difference where you live. Challenges and opportunities abound.

Wild Persimmons and Easter Freeze

OCTOBER

Persimmons are one of the great late summer–early fall delights for me and I'll bet for a bunch of you, too.

Part of my birding operation during persimmon-ripening season in northwest Arkansas involves the location of trees that ripen earlier than others. They ripen WAY, WAY before any kind of "typical" late fall–early winter freeze. It's fun to eat a few persimmons while looking for the late migrating tanagers. Looking for just the right RIPE persimmon provides a good excuse to look around the field for that odd, perched sparrow. Sampling these potentially ripe persimmons also may have drawbacks—most of you know—puckered mouth.

After the first few freezes, there are usually lots of persimmons available in all of the old field and abandoned farm fields where I like to go birding in the Fayetteville area. Persimmons are, ecologically-speaking, an early successional species. They begin to take over in the fencerow and the abandoned field. It's a good place to look for bobwhites. I see all kinds of birds in early winter going after this really huge food crop. There's nothing really quite like a flock of Cedar Waxwings swarming over a bunch of persimmons.

I have been concerned because the Easter freeze of 2007 slammed all kinds of wild food crops in northwest Arkansas. There are no pawpaws this year, so far as I can see—I check the patches. And almost no persimmons.

However, I have finally found a few persimmons that seemingly escaped the freeze. I can see evolution at work in this, I think: most persimmons flower about the same time, and these trees have no fruit this year and produced no seeds. They're "normal." But I have now found a grand total of six trees with good fruit. Perhaps the timing of their flowers is just a little out-of-kilter with the persimmon mainstream, and as a result, they have survived the Easter freeze catastrophe? These "abnormal" persimmons may pass their seeds into the future, better to survive future, ill-timed freezes.

Red-shouldered Hawk perched on a clothesline pole in my Fayetteville backyard on January 9, 2006. These colorful hawks have adapted to urban forests throughout northwest Arkansas. Filmmaker Carl Hitte produced a documentary about their nesting at Wilson Park in Fayetteville.

These are ecological issues fun to think about while birding (and eating). It also gives me hope for some of us "abnormal" people.

I will share an image of waxwings porking-out on winter persimmons, if anyone is interested. It's from 2002, a "normal" year, when I first started digiscoping with a low pixel camera, and therefore of minimal quality.

Fayetteville CBC

DECEMBER 16

We held our count on Sunday, December 16. We are still reviewing a couple of birds, but the final species tally will be close to 100—excellent for northwest Arkansas and right up there with our highest tallies in the years since 1961 when this count began. Are we better birders? With better equipment? More of us? Is global warming impacting the totals? Perhaps each makes a contribution. It snowed lightly in the Fayetteville area on the fifteenth, but cleared, and the sixteenth was pretty mild and calm—as fine a winter day for a Christmas Bird Count as possible.

After the day we assembled to tally up at Doug and Elizabeth James's home, as usual. The two birds that got the most attention were Short-eared Owl found by James Morgan's group (a first for our count and rare overall in our area) and a Spotted Towhee found by Mike Mlodinow's group (a fifth record for the Fayetteville CBC; photographed by Jacque Brown). In choosing the most charismatic bird of the day, the assembled group split toward the owl. Richard Stauffacher, an artist and long time CBCer, donated a Great Blue Heron etching as reward for this discovery.

Jason Lucier's group of graduate students found two American Tree Sparrows. Roland Roth, one of Doug James's former students who is now himself retired from teaching birds, also found a tree sparrow.

Our group had a fine day at the University farm, just north of the campus: pipits pipits pipits everywhere, a flock of 12 Horned Larks and a small flock of 6 Lapland Longspurs, and billions of Savannah Sparrows. We expect or reasonably hope for each of these, but extreme weather north and west of us swelled these numbers. I wonder what we missed? Where was that Snow Bunting? That Rough-legged Hawk? That . . . ? (sigh)

We all have "good" birds that "get away," and my group had one for sure. We were in a big grassy field sorting through Song, Swamp, and Savannah Sparrows, hunting for bobwhites and Le Conte's. Suddenly we saw an immature Bald Eagle floating over us. While watching it, another bird, much further away, flew across our field of view. It was large, long-necked, short tailed, a kind of dove gray color except for darker areas in the primaries. The wing beat was rapid, unlike a Great Blue, and its straight neck flight was also wrong for a Great Blue. It was a ???.

I wanted it to be a Sandhill Crane, but others at our tally later thought it more likely a swan. Standing in the field, knowing it was getting away, I longed for my spotting scope and a closer view. Still I am glad for these tantalizing moments, these fleeting glances, these great surprises, even if we don't cinch the ID. There's next year, god willing, and a perhaps a diagnostic view.

But why be greedy here? So many birds, so many diagnostic views of our universe's amazing diversity, so many gestures and hints about what we have inherited, and for what we are responsible. It reminds me of something from the Psalms of my Southern Baptist upbringing in Fort Smith: "This is the day that the lord hath made and I will rejoice and be glad in it."

After **NOT** IDing the Tantalizing Bird, we had close views of a dark Harlan's Hawk that Roland spotted.

—Joe Neal, Fayetteville CBC compiler and
owner-upper for that one that got away.

2008

Lake Fayetteville View

NOVEMBER 28

I went out to Lake Fayetteville early Thanksgiving, a brilliant, warm day of glasslike water. From the top of the dam, on the north shore, an adult Bald Eagle; along the south shore, 7 waterfowl. The sun illuminated the heads of a few of these birds. Eventually I could see reddish shaggy crests of Red-breasted Mergansers. Two Ring-billed Gulls flew over.

My eyeball was pushed into the scope when a familiar voice greeted me. "Whatcha seeing, Joe?" It was Wade Caldwell, a local scout leader and member of the City of Fayetteville's parks committee. He was on a bike, and with some other folks, on a Thanksgiving morning ride. I spotted a Common Loon as he came up.

Caldwell has been involved with scouting for years. The trail that now entirely loops Lake Fayetteville was initiated as a scout project. I told him that Doug James and his students birded the lake in the 1950s, when it was brand new and of course trail-less, and when much of the shoreline was without trees and visited by migrating yellowlegs. Caldwell and the scouts are now hard at work on a seven-mile loop trail around Lake Sequoyah, also in Fayetteville.

Parts of the Lake Fayetteville trail have been paved, making it highly accessible for those with walking impairments. You can park at or near the marina, and wheel with no barriers all the way across the dam—with a look at all the lake's deepwater (loon, merganser, gulls, eagle, etc) and keep rolling to the forested stream bottom at the spillway, crossed by a magnificent pedestrian bridge with a fine view into the crowns of soaring sycamores. You can run, walk the dog, push a stroller or a wheelchair, or just saunter and sit, like me with my scope.

The loop trail, and now its paved accessible sections, testifies to public-spirited civic activism joined with government action aimed at improving opportunities for all. It's a reality for which I truly give thanks, and I thanked Wade Caldwell for his vision and work.

With some more study, I figured-out the 7 birds were 3 Red-breasted Mergansers, plus 4 Common Goldeneyes—first of the season for me.

"I have great faith in a seed. Convince me that you have a seed there, and I am prepared to expect wonders."—H. D. Thoreau

2009

The Great Pruning: Ice Storm of Late January

JANUARY 31 AND FEBRUARY 1

Northwest Arkansas isn't as iced-in today as it was on Tuesday and Wednesday. Still, trees and shrubs have a destroyed look. Big trees in my yard are stripped and toothpicklike. I now live in a toothpick neighborhood.

I was out and about on Wednesday, at the height of the ice. There was an Orange-crowned Warbler at my feeder—a first for me. There is a persimmon tree in my neighborhood that I have walked by for years, and often enjoyed the persimmons. On Tuesday it was the turn of American Robins, Cedar Waxwings, and European Starlings. The top of this tree—as is the case of many trees here now—was busted out and there was a big persimmon crop on the ice. The robins spent most of their time chasing down persimmons on the ground. There was just about every robin age class you could image, and easy to watch, I suppose because hunger made them less wary. I always enjoy robins like that, but the big show involved waxwings. They swarmed persimmons hanging on branches. There were waxwings right side up, upside down, sideways, working persimmons, their bills all with persimmon globs. Somehow it reminded me of Audubon's flock of Carolina Parakeets, and of course the waxwings too are colorful and flockish, like parakeets were said to have been. Like the robins, they were less wary than usual, so I managed to collect a lot of close images.

Of course, I haven't seen them yet, because I am still without power and am on a borrowed computer. Oh, starlings: also enjoying persimmons, and all starry like they are spose to be.

Cedar Waxwing enjoying persimmons during ice-storm event at Fayetteville, January 2009.

I have a name for our now, just-about-all-gone northwest Arkansas ice storm: the great pruning. It has pruned just everything. I went to the old Lindsey Prairie today at Siloam Springs. The former prairie is covered with melted ice water. All the low places are playas. Saw 7 Bald Eagles in a field, gathered around remains of a small carcass—maybe an ice victim—seemed to be taking turns picking at what was left. Tall prairie mounds north of the Siloam airport offer refuge from the ice melt—saw 2 coyotes enjoying themselves on the east side of a big mound, in bright sunshine. One of them was darker than any coyote I've seen.

Just down the road—a fine Harlan's Hawk, perfect blotches like the cover image on the current issue of *Birding*. Hailing from the Far North, you know a big hawk like that probably wasn't too inconvenienced by the ice or the great pruning. The great pruning laid down the tall grasses at Chesney Prairie Natural Area. Swamp Sparrows there probably appreciate more water. I was watching them, then overhead heard a familiar gabbling overhead—a flock of maybe 100 Snow Geese (blues and whites), heading north. What the heck, it was sixty degrees and the sky was pure blue—maybe they were missing winter.

Bubba and the Grebe

JANUARY 25

I had a disagreeable experience birding today and wanted to share it, mainly to just vent . . . the locale is Beaver Lake in northwest Arkansas. I was up there with Amy Edie and wanting to show her the Western Grebe I had seen several times recently from Slate Gap Road near Lost Bridge. I had excitedly counted up to 162 Horned Grebes (and anticipated other water bird species as I scanned and counted). A bass boat came barreling up on the flock, never slowed, and seemed to deliberately target rafting grebes. After putting them in flight (yee-haw!), the boat slowed . . . I saw a mangled grebe. The boat turned, pulled up next to it, and bubba fished it out of the water . . . I heard laughter and saw them grinning through my spotting scope, then tossing the bloody grebe back, like it was trash. I honked and yelled. They probably thought I was saluting their manhood.

Things like this make me despair of the human race, since I assume from the obvious insensitivity that it probably applies to more than birds. I wondered what these two guys in their twenty-thousand-dollar-plus rig would think if it were grebes in the boat, barreling down purposely on them, a rafting flock of humans . . .

I had a call at home last night about a planned "crow shoot" in a small community just southeast of Fayetteville. I wondered how the crow shooters would feel if the tables were turned. That is, if crows ran the world—or at least thought they did—and planned a "people shoot." You know, got to get rid of those people—there's just too many of them and they're eating up all of our crops, etc.

I grew up as a Southern Baptist. I am fond of reminding my fellow Arkansas natives that there is no guarantee that when they get up there to the pearly gates god will necessarily be a bubba. Maybe god will be a grebe, or perhaps a crow, or perhaps . . . any of a number of undervalued and despised creatures.

Comments on Wilson Springs

FEBRUARY 28

I woke up this morning in Fayetteville to gray skies, north wind, and snow on the ground. Could be a good birding day. Also, a good day for conservation. Michelle Viney (and her team) from Audubon Arkansas's northwest Arkansas field office (Fayetteville) teamed up with Sam's Club for a volunteer work day at the Wilson Springs property here in Fayetteville, adjacent the Sam's Club. Over the years, Mike Mlodinow and I have documented more than 120 bird species there (Bell's Vireo, Painted Bunting, American Bittern, etc.). Despite the cold, north wind and snow, there were twenty-five to thirty volunteers to help remove invasive callery pears—what is hopefully the opening effort to reclaim this former Tallgrass Prairie and Henslow's Sparrow nesting habitat.

The volunteers are women and men, youngish and oldish. All of us here in NWA have been hauling limbs for a month as a result of the ice storm. Here were the volunteers from Sam's Club anyway. What a sight it was.

Michelle asked me to make a few comments before the volunteers set off on the pear removal effort. Here's what I offered: "The history of this property is basically lost in the mist of time, so let me take you back. Native Americans hunted buffalo here. Buffalo were still seen in the Fayetteville area by the first visitors in the 1820s. The City of Fayetteville was established in Prairie Township. Please note: it was not established in Tree Township, Subdivision Township, or Mall Township, or Sam's Club Township. It was Prairie Township, because when the first settlers here looked around what they saw were tall native prairie grasses: Big Bluestem, Little Bluestem, Indian Grass, and Switch Grass. The only trees they saw were in scattered oak barrens surrounded by native grass plus trees along the major streams, like Clabber Creek.

"This is what I mean about being lost in the mist of time. You cannot look around Fayetteville now and see the buffalo or the native grasses. But, that doesn't mean history is unimportant.

"Clabber Creek and its associated natural springs is an important perennial stream that runs through what was once an extensive prairie that consisted of at least twenty-five square miles, part of which included Prairie Township. In the Clabber Creek area, open fields were covered with prairies grasses and prairie wildflowers. The fields included small round mounds—we call them prairie mounds—that formed thousands of years ago. Mounds have been mostly plowed down and paved over. The native grasses and wildflowers have been mostly replaced with non-native grasses like fescue. The fields have been invaded by non-native trees like callery pears.

"The Wilson Springs property is important because many aspects of its status as prairie grassland remain. There are still prairie mounds on the property, including fine examples near the Wilson Spring run within sight of Sam's Club. A rare prairie fish, the Arkansas Darter, can still be found in Wilson Spring. Scattered in nooks and crannies are small areas that retain the four chief native grasses: Big Bluestem, Little Bluestem, Indian Grass, and Switch Grass. Some very rare wetland plants have also survived, reminding us of our natural heritage right under our noses here alongside I-540.

"Wilson Springs is still one of the best places in the immediate Fayetteville area to see and hear more than 120 species of native birds, many of them strongly associated with prairies. Bell's Vireo, once a common bird here, still nests in the open field thickets. Painted Buntings—one of America's most beautiful native birds—occurs here in summer. Until recent years, Henslow's Sparrow found one of its only nesting habitats in Arkansas here.

"Located in the heart of the development area of northwest Arkansas, Wilson Springs provides that rare green space where people can commune with nature on her own terms near where we live the rest of our lives. Restoration efforts can improve this opportunity by returning more of Wilson Springs to its original beauty and functionality as a prairie coursed by perennial springs and Clabber Creek. This restoration will add greatly to the value of the property to all visitors, surrounding developments, and it will help rescue from the mists of time our true prairie origins in Prairie Township."

American Bittern out in the open at Red Slough on July 19, 2010.

American Bittern
with Two Legs, Two Feet

MARCH 1

I was out at Woolsey Wet Prairie in Fayetteville this morning, for about as long as I could take it: temps in twenties, north wind, water iced-over, and a thin crust of snow. Woolsey had a prescribed burn on February 20, so a lot of the tall grasses are short and black. But there are many places too wet for fire to be effective, and vegetation remained there. First thing I noticed—more meadowlarks there than I had seen before (35–40)—no doubt, taking advantage of the good foraging after the burn (I only heard Easterns). Also, maybe 15 Wilson's Snipe. Sedge Wren, 1, in sedges not much impacted. Then, suddenly, an American Bittern lifted up in front of me out of some dense vegetation between

Nelson's Sparrow at Woolsey Wet Prairie on October 10, 2008. This rare transient through northwestern Arkansas blends very well into the dense marshy vegetation where we sometimes find it.

the prairie mounds, tried to go north, then sort of drifted back low and right over me. Other than a bittern I once saw and watched in a leisurely fashion while sitting in my car at Centerton, this was one of the best looks ever. I don't think the prescribed burn hurt this bird: it clearly had both legs and both feet. There were 15–20 Swamp Sparrows, ~10 Song Sparrows, 8 White-crowned Sparrows, and a seemingly endless flock of Savannah Sparrows, which I counted up to 78.

Now for a couple of landscape comments: Behind Woolsey is Northwest Arkansas's newest mountain—it's called Mt. Limb and Tree Trunk, child of the ice storm, growing daily. Twisted limbs from all over the area are being hauled and dumped there. Quite a few are from my own yard. As fast as possible, the limbs are being returned to wood fiber by the planet's biggest wood chipper.

The prairie itself never looked more interesting: with much of the vegetation burned-off, you can clearly see the height and shape of the prairie mounds and the intermoundal playas.

Birds, Trillums, Fire

MARCH 22

After seeing the trilliums in bloom at Ninestone Land Trust on March 20, I decided to head over to Cave Springs Cave Natural Area in Benton County, to visit the mother lode of Ozark Wake Robins (*Trillium pusillum* var. *ozarkanum*). They were sure enough in bloom—thousands on a gentle north-facing slope above a cave that houses the rare Ozark Cave Fish. I was also hoping to get my first spring hearing of Black-and-white Warbler, an early parula or Yellow-throated Vireo, but struck out. The trilliums alone were worth the effort. However, I didn't go away feeling all that great about the visit . . .

Unfortunately, patches of these rare trilliums on Cave Springs Cave Natural Area are in the process of being overwhelmed and smothered by honeysuckle and other aggressive non-natives like the vine *Euonymus fortunei* (wintercreeper). The only cure for such a thing is mother nature's favorite tool, fire. Repeated winter or early spring burns, before the trilliums are up, would suppress/push back the honeysuckle and other alien plants, leaving the cherty rubble free for the emergence of trilliums and other botanicals adapted to open forest landscapes free of smotherers and stranglers like honeysuckle. Some patches have already been lost to honeysuckle and wintercreeper.

I mention this in the context of rare trilliums, because the same thing hugely impacts birds. Many among us conservationists (in our case, bird lovin'/Audubon community) still don't have the fire thing figured out—how historically fires shaped the natural landscape, and how without deliberately using fire, it will be impossible to reset the clock, even in those patches that we call preserves, natural areas, national forests, etc.

Admittedly, my attitude about this is STRONGLY shaped by years of working as a USDA Forest Service Wildlife Biologist with endangered Red-cockaded Woodpeckers, which were headed for extinction before biologists began to strongly push fire back into southern pine forests. Bobwhite quail, Bachman's Sparrows, Prairie Warblers and many other birds have rebounded in those habitats where fire is reintroduced. I saw it for myself on the Ouachita National Forest in west central Arkansas.

So, my friends in the conservation community with a worry about fire, treat yourself to a good read. The bible in this case: *Restoring North American Birds, Lessons from Landscape Ecology* by Robert A. Askins (I read the second edition).

We don't need to keep scratching our heads about this one. Just get that drip torch and go to work!

Plover-Eye View

MARCH 25

I saw American Golden-Plovers again today in a former Tallgrass Prairie area immediately south of the Craig State Fish Hatchery at Centerton, Benton County. It must be March and they must be flying in with spring. There were approximately 180 golden plovers in the southwest corner

This single American Golden-Plover was part of a flock at Centerton on March 24, 2004. Northwest Arkansas forms part of a migratory path in spring that spans ten thousand miles, with northwest Arkansas about midway.

Common Nighthawk near the Nature Conservancy's Tallgrass Prairie Preserve in northeastern Oklahoma on July 21, 2007.

of fields at Anglin and Barron Roads, plus more in adjacent fields, and 7 at the hatchery. These are all low-lying fields, with playa-like pools in places from yesterday's heavy rain. Wilson's Snipe, yellowlegs, Pectoral Sandpipers were among them in fields with dairy cows.

I am always amazed at the fantastic juxtapositions of time, place, and history. Here are the migrants of ten thousand miles, set down like magic among us. Their ancestors must have done the same when bison and prairie chickens reigned. The plovers are immaculately wild and for me the releaser from burdens of modernity among things strictly mundane. The birds give their *que-ees* calls, seemingly oblivious to traffic on Arkansas 279 and cows demanding morning hay. There were also Great-tailed Grackles there, with their fantastic *chucks* and whistles.

It's a transporting thing, being among them, with binoculars and questions. What a truly fantastic landscape, from the plover-eye view.

Ramblings from the Former Prairies of Benton County

APRIL 13

Good tidings from the former prairies of western Benton County:

I spent the last two days either birding in the rain or near it. The skies are dark and wind is northwest. While floral spring is delayed, the old former prairies are vibrant with ephemeral pools and stalled grasspipers. You can see how things used to work during spring migration through the Tallgrass Prairies of western Arkansas. Northward moving Blue-winged Teal and Northern Shovelers take advantage of the new shallow pools in the fields. Many ponds and pools have their own Greater Yellowlegs, including some small flocks. The big fields with grazers have their coterie of American Golden-Plovers. I had a conservative count this morning of 225 golden-plovers between Centerton and Vaughn (a good number for northwestern Arkansas), where flocks have been daily since at least March 21 and at least 45 at another pool just west of Hiwassee. Yesterday, in the rain, I saw 9 Upland Sandpipers standing on the partially flooded road near Vaughn. They were in the adjacent pasture today, among the grazers: they glide through the new grass, presence reduced to that large dark eye. Finally, an ultra-elegant Great Blue Heron, in nest season high finery, lord of an ephemeral pool.

I made a swing up through the Safari near Gentry, for nesting Great-tailed Grackles. Even in a cold, steady rain, His Lordships are perched, bills pointed up, atop the trees, tails curled and cocked. Below, Her Ladyship gathers bits of grass (hay) and disappears into the small dense trees, where nests are underway. His Lordship squeals, flutters, whistles, squawks so that the neighbor Lordship, two feet away, gets the message: it's all about space and the future of things.

Killdeer down on the gravel road, covering two eggs from the cold.

Woo Woo Moments
with a Very Cool Sora

APRIL 14

I spent part of today birding with Lynn Christie from Little Rock. We started out in the Vaughn area of Benton County. When we got up there it looked like most of the 200+ American Golden-Plovers had continued on their epochal ten-thousand-mile journey. We did find 6 of the original 9 in a flock of Upland Sandpipers. Just as I began making solemn pronouncements about gone plovers and their amazing odyssey, and lots of other miscellaneous stuff I've heard on PBS, here they came, in tight flocks, making a fine display. Not yet gone, a few thousand miles still left. I also pronounced 2 Blue-winged Teal on a far pond, that Lynn noticed were shovelers . . .

After Vaughn, we headed for Woolsey Wet Prairie at Fayetteville. I was telling how Joyce Shedell just saw a Sora at the Centerton hatchery (posted on ARBIRD-L), so I thought . . . well maybe we can see one today at Woolsey. After the yellowlegs, after Wilson's Snipe, after the teal (both), after avoiding a threatening Canada Goose, after a dramatic Cooper's stoop on shorebirds, etc. etc. . . . a Sora—casually it seemed— walked out of wet grass, right in front of us. It was so dramatic I could barely breathe.

OK, Sora is not a rare transient in Arkansas, BUT this Sora appeared and stopped. Didn't dodge back into cover. Didn't fly up and drop out of sight. Didn't leave me wondering if it was a Virginia Rail. Remained in plain sight and in perfect light, and stayed there for eternity. It knew we wanted it (my friend Joy Fox would call this a woo-woo moment): red eye, yellow beak, white under cocked tail, dove gray on sides, rich whites/blacks/browns of wings and back. It turned this way, then that. We got the whole thing. There's no way to have seen more. Finally it sauntered into cover. That red eye among leaves of grass.

Now at home, thinking about it, I like Peterson's Sora best, of the various bird book illustrators. But even with its high artistry, Peterson looks pretty static compared to the gaudy remarkable beauty that showed today. These are moments that made me a birder and keep me. I don't need it every time. Once in a while will keep me under the spell.

Sora at Woolsey Wet Prairie in Fayetteville April 14, 2009. These secretive rails are modestly common at times during migration, but are hard to see. But out in the open and easily seen, this Sora was an exciting exception.

Wilson's Snipe near Chesney Prairie Natural Area on April 22, 2009. Snipe are classic "grasspipers"—shorebirds that blend well into the protective cover of vegetation in wet areas.

Swainson's Thrush on Scull Creek Bike Trail

APRIL 17

I had a Swainson's Thrush singing this morning on the Scull Creek bike trail at Fayetteville. This is the typical first arrival period here (around second-third week in April). The song slowed and mesmerized me—a good thing. A few miles further—White-eyed Vireo. We do get them earlier, but this creature-gem exhibited typical arrival. I had errands to do, and heard House Wrens singing in three places, so that's starting up, too, also about on time. None of this was official "birding," but it was official "biking," happy combination: ears do the walking.

Also saw my friend Steve Erwin (of local winter Summer Tanager fame) in his Cardinals ball cap, on the trail with an armload of trash he had picked up, just because it's worthwhile. Like a favorite bumper sticker about acts of kindness, just because. Scull Creek and its creatures appreciate the less plastic just because he stooped to help.

Yesterday evening, at Lake Fayetteville, Stephanie Cribbs and I saw and heard the *reap reap* of a Great Crested Flycatcher, nonchalantly atop one of millions of damaged, broken, or uprooted trees. That date, April 16, ties the earliest previous record in northwest Arkansas as far as I know. From that trip I harvested the following (with many, many apologies to Emily Dickinson):

> To direct attention to a bird
>
> in our post ice storm age
>
> gesture toward a tree
>
> broken more or less in half.
>
> Mention bird of interest.
>
> See it's in the crown
>
> that one, upside down.
>
> Well maybe halfway or midway
>
> toward the ground . . .

Ibises in the genus *Plegadis* migrate through northwest Arkansas, like this one (of 2) seen and photographed at Centerton on October 14, 2009.

Our World Needs Its Ibises and Gallinules

APRIL 20

I went birding yesterday in a key part of the Little River Bottoms Important Bird Area in southwestern Arkansas near Lake Millwood. My partners and guides were Charles Mills and Yancey Reynolds, both long

Flock of White-faced Ibises, state fish hatchery at Centerton on May 8, 2005.

time members of Arkansas Audubon Society. Water birds, water birds, everywhere; a partial list: Anhinga (nesting), Great Egret (nesting), Snowy Egret (nesting), Tricolored Heron (3–4 birds), Black-crowned Night-herons, White Ibis (big flocks, hadn't started yet to nest, but immaculate!), Bald Eagle (nesting), Purple Gallinule (2 seen), Common Moorhen (abundant, wonderfully vocal), Prothonotary Warblers singing from cypress everywhere. This IBA is the finest imaginable expression of Arkansas's aquatic ecosystems.

Within a few miles is the site for a proposed coal-fired electrical generating plant. Southwest Arkansas has a lot of human poverty and a remarkable natural heritage. Many needed jobs are promised and so the coal plant has local support, but also Jeremiahs. Many of you know Charles Mills and his remarkable, scientific and highly artistic photography of birds, dragonflies, etc. On the way back, I asked him if he had ever had a public exhibit of his photography. No (a few prairie wildflowers appeared in one show). To me it brings focus.

An accomplished regional artist is uncelebrated in his backyard;

the coal plant is greeted with hosannas. The desire for jobs and a better material life are completely understandable amidst great poverty. Yes, we energy hogs (like me) need electricity. But, in our greed, we trade natural heritages for chimeras. Bring us the women and men in political life who will step up to the need to provide healthy opportunity to those who have been left behind and combine that with understanding that our world is fatally flawed without its ibises and gallinules.

Cheery Bend

MAY 6

Judith Ann Griffith and I birded in Madison and Franklin Counties May 6, mainly between Brashears (intersection Highways 16 and 23, aka the "pig trail") and Cass (on 23). I met Judith at Brashears. At the start, we were in our local cloud forest. Through the fine mist we could hear both Sedge and Marsh Wrens in a big hayfield and soon had both in close view. I had already seen a first year male Orchard Oriole atop a brush pile. When we returned in the afternoon, two Bobolinks perched atop the brush and nearby was a flock of 10 Orchard Orioles.

The main focus was Cherry Bend in the Ozark National Forest. It's half-way between Brashears and Cass and involves about two miles of upper, east-facing moist, mature hardwood slope. We parked in the small lot where the Ozark Highlands Trail crosses 23, then walked up to Rock House, which overlooks slopes below.

We saw bunting flocks along the whole drive between Brashears and Cass, in both the private farmland and National Forest. Most involved 5–10 Indigos in all plumages, a few had 25 or so, and some included a few White-crowned and Chipping Sparrows. At Cass, we saw a fine male Painted Bunting along the roadside. We got the red around the eyes, both greens, etc. I cannot imagine what the field and thicket-loving White-crowned Sparrows felt when they awoke midst the shagbark hickories and pawpaws of Cherry Bend!

In the Cherry Bend area we made several short stops and listens, and the short hike up from the parking lot to Rock House. The native

Marsh Wren in thicket of bur-marigold flowers at Lake Sequoyah on October 2, 2005. Richard Stauffacher and I canoed out into the lake to see American White Pelicans and found this bird on a low island with a good view of the pelicans.

wild azaleas are blooming and it's hard not to stop in full-blown admiration for a fine male Black-throated Green Warbler when you have a flaming pink bush extending over a high bluff, and below, the stream full and screaming. At Rock House we caught a crack of sunlight and at eye level a singing male Cerulean Warbler. For those of us mainly used to butt shots of Ceruleans high in the canopy, an eye level male in decent light makes clear the bird's name and its unique creation. I was just dumbstruck and that's saying something in my case. We humans have fine sensibilities, but they can be overloaded.

For the day, we recorded 21 warbler species. In the forests at Cherry Bend, we had the following: Golden-winged (1), Tennessee, Nashville, Chestnut-sided, Black-throated Green (in four spots; they are likely breeding birds at Cherry Bend now), Cerulean (12, all along the two miles and best place I know in the Ozarks), Black-and-white, American Redstart, Worm-eating, Ovenbird, Kentucky, Hooded, Wilson's. These are mostly common breeding birds at Cherry Bend.

Also at Cherry Bend, our highway workers are valiantly repairing giant cracks and minislides in the asphalt. Bless their hearts; it's a critical road through our neck of the woods. Gravity makes its claims on highways, just as it does on us. Judith and I made our way carefully along 23, spotting Swainson's Thrushes and one Gray-cheeked Thrush using roadsides. This old "pig trail" is steadily heading downhill and one senses it has chosen return to its pre-1880 state as a pioneer trail and Native American hunting track. We have smart highway folks and I'll bet they can keep it going for us who love birding and botanizing Cherry Bend, not to mention all the Ozark towns and communities who depend upon the feed trucks and freighters passing through, below Rock House, where we are watching Ceruleans and wondering at the many Hoodeds . . . and the virtually unimaginable resplendence of Scarlet Tanagers in spring light.

Cherry Bend was a "cheery" place today. I thank Jacque Brown for choosing to call this place "Cheery Bend."

Western Benton County for International Migratory Bird Day

MAY 9

It rained all night Friday night, but when I got up Saturday morning . . . lo, darkness had turned to light, the storm had cleared, and there was a promising north breeze. How much more perfect could it be? No way to order up more perfect weather for finding migrants! Highlights:

Grounded flocks of Eastern Kingbirds, Orchard Orioles, Baltimore Orioles, with Dickcissels and Indigo Buntings mixed in various numbers. This is my second International Migratory Bird Day to see grounded orioles in front of a north breeze. Maybe grounded and exhausted— relatively many Painted Buntings, too, in places I'm not used to seeing them later—

American Bittern at Stump Prairie, flushed from a shallow pool of native Cordgrass, Bell's Vireo singing away in the native indigo bushes above—thank you Joe Woolbright for ten years of backbreaking and often

Hudsonian Godwit (upturned bill), Stilt Sandpiper (down-turned bill) at University farm in Fayetteville on International Migratory Bird Day May 14, 2005. We don't often get to directly compare the stunning, highly evolved bills side-by-side as was the case on this day.

thankless restoration work making this habitat attractive to its natives—I thought of you and others like you as I watched the bittern—

Clay-colored Sparrows—found them in three places, and in two watched them singing or buzzing to be more specific—7 total was my "conservative" count, though instinct tells me the number was at least two times that—

Black-bellied Plover—a single bird, fully decked out in to-die-for breeding plumage, in a big young bean field, dwarfing a Killdeer that maybe didn't want it there—singing Horned Larks, maybe in accompaniment?

Swainson's Hawk—not unexpected at Maysville, but sure good to see for **IMBD**—two adults soaring together, then a third bird, or was it one of these 2?—over the old Beaty Prairie with breeze under wings . . .

Bewick's Wren (brown back, eastern form): just as I was ready to throw in the towel, I heard Bewick's Wren singing from a yard—one of those yards full of cars, trucks, storage sheds, all paraphernalia of family life in the Arkansas back country. How weird and suspicious a "big city" (**AKA,** Fayetteville) birder looks, all bined-out and such, hot on the trail of a what (?) a wren? Why? What do you want? But invariably and generously, the waters part, incredulity gives way to interest and I get permission to stalk their yard. Bless their hearts.

What a weird and sometimes very wonderful world is this in which we live.

Barred Owl fledgling, just off the nest in a broken-off top of a
mature oak at Lake Fayetteville, May 6, 2005.

Erbie on the Buffalo River

MAY 16

The Disorganized Birder's Club (DOBS) of Harrison sponsored a field
trip for members and visitors May 16, to Erbie along the Buffalo National
River. We met in the rain at the Koen Forest Trail, just north of Jasper.
In the rain we saw both tanager species, and as the rain lifted, we had
warblers, including Blackburnian, Blackpoll, and others. There are tulip
poplars along the trail, and they were in full bloom, amazing flowers

attended by Baltimore Orioles, plumage a nice match with orange in the petals. It dazzled me, watching them way-way up there, until my neck hurt and I had to keep wiping the old bins . . . it's a world we barely enter, but I rejoice at least such peaks.

Jack Stewart (Arkansas Audubon Society president and expert birder) was our leader and he treated us to a hike on the "Erbie loop" he and Pam walk from their home just above the Buffalo valley. Highlights of the loop: Blue-winged Warblers in the pioneer-era like forest openings (park service keeps them open with prescribed burning, like in "ye olden days") and a fine Swainson's Warbler that sang in the open for us along the edge of a huge river cane thicket along the Buffalo. David Oakley got some bell ringer-type photos of the singing bird.

There were also some wonderful, mysterious *gwaks* that we decided must be a Yellow-crowned Night-Heron, but who knows. The universal merry prankster may have been using Her MP3 player . . . such mystery provides refreshment for our besotted minds to play and wander. Thank you, universe.

We visited the Stewarts in their "off the grid" home, but not before great looks at Prairie Warblers in the field we walked through. "Off the grid"—we saw the solar generation set up that powers their modern lifestyle (lights, computers, TV, etc.). It was looking at the future and having a chance to be there, where the whole country must head in the coming years, in some shape and form, though perhaps not as serene and fetching as this modern cabin above the valley of the Buffalo National River.

Mourning Warblers and Former Prairies

MAY 26

In writing about Mourning Warblers in the Birds of North America series, Jay Pitocchelli states that it is a common breeder in cleared but regenerating areas of North America's boreal forest, winters in Central and South America, where it also prefers disturbed areas with thick undergrowth. He also says that in favoring such clearings caused by logging or forest fires, this warbler may be one of North America's few Neotropical migrants that has benefited from human settlement.

I mention this because Jacque Brown, David Oakley, and I found a fine singing male at Chesney Prairie Natural Area yesterday (May 25) in just such circumstances—a thicket along a regenerating tree line in the headwaters of Sager Creek. Both of them obtained prize-winning images. It was the kickoff of a fascinating, rainy spring day on the former prairie lands in western Benton County.

I use the term former prairies because almost all Tallgrass Prairie habitat in northwestern Arkansas was long ago plowed and planted to introduced grasses, massively altering their botanical character. Nevertheless, the clay-rich soils remain, and because of that—and because prairie plants are tenacious—the former prairies retain many important aspects of their histories—and some of its bird life.

From Chesney, we drove the mile or so to Stump Prairie. First we heard a Bell's Vireo in a prairie wetland thicket (mostly indigo bush), audible above traffic on Highway 59. The first bird we saw was an adult Swainson's Hawk, on the ground in a recently mowed pasture, consuming what we eventually decided was a rabbit, probably killed or injured in the mowing. You could hear the cameras firing away on that one. When the bird made a slow, low loop over us, an Oakley whoop easily topped feed trucks on 59.

We found two of the region's prize prairie orchids in bloom: ragged orchid *Platanthera lacera* and grass pink orchid *Calopogon tuberosus*. Joe Woolbright, land steward for both these special areas, told us about the flowers. He was off working on a project near Sulphur Springs where yesterday he found more rare plants! The areas where we found both orchids both had spring prescribed burns this year.

One of the real gems of these open country fencerows, thickets, and shrublands are Painted Buntings. We had at least 4 during the day. Over the years I have come to the conclusion that the more open the area—that is, the more it resembles a prairie—the more likely we find Painteds, even if Indigo Buntings are nearby and plentiful. Conversely, the more forest habitat develops (especially with effective fire control), the better the habitat becomes for Indigos. If we are to bring back Painteds, getting fire back into these habitats is the key.

Shaping-in-the-Making

JUNE 26

Cooper's Hawk was common in the Fayetteville area in the '50s, rare at least by the late '70s. It is now **VERY BACK** as a nester. I share the expressed joy of William Shepherd and others posting to this list on recovery. It is easy to be so overwhelmed by negative in our world that we fail to celebrate concrete evidence that sound science backing thoughtful public policy can make it better.

Historically—northwestern Arkansas probably had a nesting population of Upland Sandpipers on its Tallgrass Prairies. We still see them regularly as transients. Rose Ann Barnhill, David Oakley, Jacque Brown, and I made a trip over to the Tallgrass Prairie Preserve north of Tulsa on June 20. We were treated to dozens of Upland Sandpipers that nest there. A trip like that is time travel. We are back to Arkansas in 1800. We saw 5 ornate box turtles, another amazing creature mostly lost to Arkansans. Finding one is like finding an arrowhead. Others have been here before.

We had a field trip over to Baker Prairie with the Disorganized Birder's Club in Harrison on June 13, expressly to seek Willow Flycatchers. This is the only bird first described to science from Arkansas. In Audubon's time, they were apparently widespread nesting birds on our prairies. Slowly our prairies have disappeared, as have nesting Willow Flycatchers. We found them on June 13, and Leesia Marshall-Rosenberger showed us a nest. This is the only place in the state (I think) where they still nest. We were as excited as Audubon, when he saw his first.

The situation with Cooper's Hawk, Upland Sandpiper, and Willow Flycatcher reminds me of how we shape the environment, good and ill. Shaping is all around us. The proposed coal plant down by Grassy Lake and Lake Millwood is a shaping-in-the-making. As in the case of hawks, sandpipers, and flycatchers—we have choices to make. It is about how many watts to generate and how to generate. We have futures to shape. It is about the nature of power.

Some of y'all got upset when some others celebrated the recent court decision rethinking the coal project. As I write on my computer, cooled by AC, with cold water in the ice box (oops, refrigerator), I am reminded we don't have a realistic choice about whether or not to generate electricity. That train has already left the station. But how—is that not the CURRENT question?

If you look at the billions of folks in the developing world who are just now learning to depend on lights and fans, it is easy enough to see our planetary distress. We need electricity generated in a way that guides the world, as we aspire to do with democracy. I would very much like to see our large utilities lead in generating power. I mean it metaphorically. They have the people, the expertise, and the resources IF we want it.

Creating jobs folks desperately need in southwest Arkansas— YES. Generating electricity that reflects the needs of our future— YES. Retooling America to help us lead the world in a safer cleaner energy future—YES. That is POWER, thoughtful and respectful of our future.

We can bring back Cooper's Hawk, and we can restore more of our Tallgrass Prairie plus the wonderful creatures that require it. We can have electricity, jobs, ornate box turtles, and a relatively clean environment. We do not have to live in negativity and refusal to celebrate the good and the possible, just because it is different than practices in the past or not as perfect as we wish it could be.

I am proud to say: we lead the world in many aspects of living, and we do it in thoughtful, respectful conservation as well.

Christian Conservative Birders

JULY 1

Off and on over the last couple of years, I have conversed via email and in person or gone birding with LOTS of Christian Conservative Birders (CCBs) plus some of what I assume are Christian Liberal Birders. I am TOTALLY comfortable with CCBs, having grown up as a CC myself in Fort Smith, before I was a B. I still identify myself as a Southern Baptist, though mainly in a cultural sense; I love the hymns, the communities, and of course many of my relatives who still believe as we did in our youth. What I no longer do is embrace the social and political agendas of the noisier Christian Conservatives.

Looking back, I realize this noisy C agenda is not a new thing.

When I was a kid in Fort Smith, we were taught from the pulpit, Holy Bible in hand, that African Americans who were kneeling-in at Southern Baptist churches to promote racial diversity within those churches were Communists, not real Christians. We were taught that if the Catholic John Kennedy was elected, America would be ruled by a foreign Pope. And so on. I still have a deadly fear of drinking beer on Sundays and I am sometimes suspicious of Methodists (just kidding!).

As a young college student (UA Fayetteville-1964), I began to see the world through different eyes, politically and socially. That said, I have never felt a need to reject the morals, values, and spiritual teachings of my parents. As I formulated my own beliefs, I no longer embraced that an Immaculate Conception was required for human beings to have divine spark. I was also taught and never rejected that the right to think for yourself is the best of our American values. Those who think America needs "ayatollahs" and religious laws (to replace elected Presidents and a civil constitution) really should try at least a brief residence in one of those countries run that way AND perhaps take a deep bath in the history of our own country and its founding. I have taught my daughter to respect faith and seek the truth of things in her day-to-day living.

So, I enjoy birding with people of traditional faith, whatever that faith, Conservative or Liberal, or Neither, including no belief. As a (I

American Goldfinch harvesting thistles in Clabber Creek bottomlands in
Fayetteville, August 1, 2004. They delay nesting until thistle down is available
as nest material. American Goldfinch is the symbol of Northwest Arkansas
Audubon Society.

guess) Liberal Birder, I personally welcome all of Christian Conservative
Birders to this list, to their faith, and to field trips. Please miss your usual
Sunday morning services and join our congregation at Chesney Prairie
on July 12, 8 a.m., for services at Birdside Baptist.

Every Baptist preacher worth his salt knows it is a mortal sin to let
divine services spill over and cut into the Sunday noon feast. We will
end services by noon, I promise.

Black-bellied Whistling-Ducks near Frog Bayou WMA on July 11, 2009.

Arkansas River Sandbars

JULY 15

Richard Stauffacher and I put a canoe in on the Arkansas River July 15, just south of Mulberry and Dyer, near a long string of predominantly sandy islands, and approximately a mile or so upriver from the islands we had paddled around July 8. Great Egrets still have active nests in low willow trees, though all of the nestlings visible from the boat were crawling around the nests. The apparently long string of sandy islands will be one as river levels drop.

From the canoe we saw Least Terns on three of these low sandy islets, always where there are mounds on the islands covered with pebbles (so nesting sort of like Killdeer); about 25 terns air mobile at one point. Unlike last week, we saw few brownish youngsters running about; some birds were apparently incubating. We also saw some obvious courtship, including the tern's habit of presumptive Mr. offering

Nestling Cattle Egrets on a sand island in the Arkansas River near Mulberry on July 15, 2009.

presumptive Ms. an offering—presumptive he standing erect with the long silver minnow, she crouching adjacent (but, according to rules of this list—no sex, no religion, no politics—we now modestly avert our eyes . . .).

The shallow islands also hosted shorebirds: we saw both yellowlegs (1 each), 4 Stilt Sandpipers, 5 Semipalmated Sandpipers, and 2 Spotted Sandpipers, and a couple that got away. A brilliant Baltimore Oriole chased a Fish Crow from a tall sycamore on one island. Bell's Vireos (3 in one spot) were singing with considerable vigor in the early succession vegetation near the shoreline.

On the drive back, along a two-track trace through a beanfield, 2 Horned Larks, including one singing away, oblivious to 98 degrees, bright sun, mid-July.

Black-Bellied Plover, Hiroshima, Nagasaki

AUGUST 9

Jacque Brown, David Oakley, and I spent Sunday morning, August 9, in the Arkansas River valley, in the vicinity of the University of Arkansas vegetable experiment farm and a private sod farm southeast of Kibler in Crawford County. We saw a Black-bellied Plover still in immaculate nesting plumage, plus a good sprinkling of other migrating shorebirds: Semipalmated Plover (4), Greater Yellowlegs (2), Solitary Sandpiper (6), Spotted (1), Upland (8, including 1 flock of 6), Semipalmated (1 +; many peeps), Least (2 +), Pectoral Sandpiper (24 +); 8–10 Horned Larks and a similar number of Lark Sparrows, both either at the sod farm or alongside sandy roads through bean fields (including yoy [young of the year]), Grasshopper Sparrow (1 adult singing, 2 yoy near, at sod), Painted Bunting (1; yoy), and BIG flocks of Dickcissels in the bean and sorghum fields.

At one point a couple of guys in a flatbed work truck hailed us to a stop. They explained that there were vandalism problems in the area, including folks stealing watermelons. Our bins and floppy hats marked us as potentially weird but probably harmless. It was Sunday morning,

Lark Sparrow harvesting grass seed near Centerton on July 18, 2004.

after all, and real bad guys would be shacked-up somewhere or out stealing offering plates. They had five just-picked big melons on the flatbed. After a friendly talk, they gave us directions we needed. In five minutes we spotted a watermelon that had rolled off the truck and split open blocking the roadway. There was no putting that one back together again. It was good!

We left by noon, because of heat, and because I wanted to get back to Fayetteville and still have a little August energy to see some public art: the Quaker-sponsored exhibit "Eyes wide open" displayed at the Fulbright Peace Fountain on the U of A campus PLUS to attend a program marking the anniversary of atomic bombings of Hiroshima and Nagasaki at one of the chapels adjacent campus. My dad was on a Navy ship in the Pacific ready for the invasion of Japan when the bombs were dropped. He always credited the bombs with saving his life and, by the way, getting him home soon, resulting in me. "Eyes wide open" features combat boots arranged in symmetric rows for U.S. servicemen from

Arkansas killed in more recent wars and civilian shoes in another area honoring dead non-combatants. It was honorable and sobering, even to a devout bird watcher. My own eyes and head were still wide open to Black-bellied Plovers and sudden materializations of Upland Sandpipers and generally to the timeless wonder of massive continent-wide bird movements. Thinking of my dad, birds, all of these war dead, seemed a confluence of modernity, even on campus, as we honored the disparate victims of various species of spectacular orgasmic violence.

Birdside Baptist

AUGUST 22

The following is all completely true. I am not trying to re-ignite the "culture wars."

Jacque Brown, David Oakley, and I birded in the Arkansas River bottomlands, including Frog Bayou WMA and east toward the turf farm and fields south of Kibler. We saw two adult Black-bellied Whistling-Ducks with a brood of half-grown young at the Alma sewer plant. There were Caspian and Least Terns on the Arkansas River; also 10 cormorants (which have been there all summer). Shorebirds were sparse, but we found 3 singleton Upland Sandpipers and two Buff-breasted Sandpipers. A shrike south of Alma had hung mouse, cicada, and grasshopper on barbed wire. Bell's Vireos were still singing at Frog. Yellow Warblers seemed numerous (5–10) in the bushy edge at Frog. We saw two green Painted Buntings.

While we were watching Horned Larks and the Buff-breasted Sandpipers from a graveled road that was open, well-traveled, and NOT posted, we were accosted by a gentleman who informed us we were on private land and we weren't welcome. He said some birdwatchers had found an abandoned Bald Eagle nest nearby and the government had taken forty acres of private land as a result. He asked a lot of questions, including whether or not we were Christians. He relaxed when we testified to our faith—especially brightening when I responded that

I was, like him, a Southern Baptist—and said we could keep watching. Sure glad we aren't just a bunch of bird-watchin' heathens! Today was a Saturday; we'd been in a bad way if it was Sunday.

When my sister misses Sunday morning services and instead enjoys preaching on the radio, she refers to this as attending "bedside Baptist." I guess, if we get accosted on a Sunday morning, we may claim to be attending "Birdside Baptist."

Rough-legged Hawks and Climate Change

NOVEMBER 28

The current issue of *Birding* (American Birding Association, November 2009) includes on page 35 a summary of the best current data suggesting how climate change is impacting winter bird distribution. I was delighted that the entire article appeared in the 109th Christmas Bird Count issue of *American Birds* (vol. 63) mailed to everyone who participated in last year's CBC. One of the things that caught my attention in the latter is on page 13. There are figures based upon the CBC data we all go out and collect for Rough-legged Hawk, Purple Finch, Stellar's Jay, and Carolina Wren. The figures display changes in latitudinal center of abundance during CBC periods and this is plotted against regional population trends.

I've been wondering about why we almost never see Rough-legged Hawks in Arkansas in winter anymore. Based upon figure 3, an obvious reason is that starting in the mid-1970s, the winter center of abundance for rough-legs shifted way, way north of Arkansas; it is actually now in Canada in early winter. There's something similar in Purple Finch, though the shift is not so dramatic. This stuff is all well worth a look, especially if you are personally wondering what the climate change issue is about.

This stuff was running in the back of my mind yesterday, especially, because Jacque Brown, David Oakley, and I made a tiring but birdy trip over to the Nature Conservancy's Tallgrass Prairie Preserve (TGPP, near Pawhuska, north of Tulsa). It's about three hours from the Fayetteville area. Once inside the imposing bison fences, about the first bird we saw was a light morph Rough-legged Hawk. It was zoomed by an almost pure black bird that we soon realized was a dark morph Rough-leg. Before the end of the day, we saw at least 5, and maybe as many as 9, Rough-legs. David and Jacque got wonderful images of both morphs. In one spot, Rough-legs were using an updraft of breeze against a low hill to hang almost still in the wind. We also found Smith's Longspur in 4–5 Aristida grass patches, Sprague's Pipits in a bare spot where bison gather, and Greater Prairie-Chicken and a Short-eared Owl snug down out of the wind in knee high grasses and forbs.

Perhaps rough-legs are still present at TGPP because the habitat is of such high quality, whereas areas with margin quality habitat (like the former Tallgrass Prairies in northwestern Arkansas) cannot support them in this era of changing climate . . . or something . . .

Prairie-Chickens and Bison Dung

DECEMBER 16

Someone recently told me there are prairie-chickens in Arkansas. This came from a "good source." It's one of those deathless rumors. I like it, but I doubt it.

When I was kid growing up in Fort Smith, my dad, a disabled Navy vet, worked for the Army at Fort Chaffee. We went out there to see the doctor, shop in the PX, etc. Nobody was a bird watcher in my family, and we never took time to look at birds on the base. As an adult, with my folks both gone, I have been back at Chaffee, working on a research project (1980s) involving bobwhite quail and later to see Smith's Longspur. This was a field trip on November 13, 2004, with Mike Mlodinow, Sandy Berger, and Karen McGee. Smith's country at Chaffee looks like the flint hills prairies of northeastern Oklahoma where there are sure enough prairie-chickens.

Chaffee is part of the old Massard Prairie, described by Nuttall in

Greater Prairie-Chicken "booming" from atop a pile of bison dung at the Nature Conservancy's Tallgrass Prairie Preserve in northeastern Oklahoma on April 21, 2006. Bison, prairie-chickens, and other native animal and plant species are targets of recovery efforts on the preserve.

his travels through western Arkansas Territory in 1819. So back to the claimed rediscovery of Arkansas prairie-chickens. Artillery and all other kinds of ordinance have been fired there since World War II. As a result of regular wildfires, Chaffee probably has the best and most extensive native grassland in the state, BUT you can't get into most of it—all that unexploded ordinance and—now with the unending War on Terror— all that fresh layer of security.

So I was asked about those prairie-chickens lately, and I said, "I doubt it." I regret to say, in this regard, that I sound like a poor echo of the Ivory-bill doubters. Show me the chickens and I will convert. What's most likely is some kind of exotic introduced grouse or so I was told by someone knowledgeable about the situation.

I have been thinking about this because of a field trip to TNC's Tallgrass Prairie Preserve just north of Pawhuska, Oklahoma April 20–21, 2006. Joe Woolbright set up this trip. I got to go as a bird guide. Harvey Payne, who founded the preserve and became its director,

Richard Stauffacher and Irene Camargo at the Nature Conservancy's Tallgrass Prairie Preserve in northeastern Oklahoma on April 3, 2004. We hoped to see prairie-chickens, Short-eared Owls, and other prairie species—and weren't disappointed!

guided us out to a prairie-chicken lek. Chickens boomed from the only high places available—big piles of bison dung. It could very well have been exactly the same thing on the Massard Prairie in 1819.

I wistfully doubt the reports of Greater Prairie-Chickens at Chaffee. But, if by some miracle, they survive there, I hope the unexploded ordinance and the War on Terror continues to protect them. I also hope none of the big energetic male chickens hop up heedlessly on a still viable artillery shell fuse, which may be all that's available during courtship, since there is no bison herd, or at least none reported at Chaffee—as far as I have heard.

Less Shopping, More Protecting

DECEMBER 19

Back in 2000 I saw a Red-tailed Hawk nest in the stout fork of a big old prairie-era post oak. The oak was part of a small forest developed on former Tallgrass Prairie habitat well marked by impressive prairie mounds. There were Northern Bobwhites in the surrounding fields and Painted Buntings in the shrublands. Visitors to northwest Arkansas and us locals are invariably drawn to this area now because it is Steel Creek Crossing in the burgeoning retail-entertainment district in the vicinity of Northwest Arkansas Mall. There was a big battle over these old prairie oaks in 2000, begun when Mary Lightheart climbed what she called the "mother tree" and vowed to stay until development plans were dropped. She kept her vow to stay, but eventually law enforcement brought her down and arrested others who tried to take her place.

I was out Christmas shopping in that area yesterday. What remains of that old oak barren is a handful of fantastic mature native trees and prairie mounds between two popular retailers, Kohl's and Target. Kohl's refused to make any compromise with their store building plans at the time. Folks who supported Lightheart handed out bumper stickers after the fracas that read, "I will never shop at Kohl's." Trash from the parking lots collects there, mute witness to what happens when a worthwhile fight is lost.

I haven't seen one of those "I'll never shop . . ." adorning a bumper in a few years, so I guess this too has now largely faded. Just from an ecological viewpoint, the little remnant is worth a visit because it is a perfect example of a unique Ozark habitat once much more widespread in northwestern Arkansas. There's plenty of parking nearby, too.

But I am a historian and a birder, and when I'm out that way, I always stop and look at the oaks and the mounds, remembering that big hawk nest, the bobwhites, and buntings. Bobwhites and Painted Buntings are two of our native birds whose declines are thought by some to be a mystery. Stop by the little woodlot. The reason for decline, at least in our western Arkansas neck-of-the-woods, is palpable.

I also notice that while I did, and do, support the notion of

White-throated Sparrow on December 26, 2005 in Fayetteville.

boycotting environmental travesty, like others here, I move on. It's like being pushed out to sea by the rip tide. The people who work in Kohl's and Target look and likely feel just like you and me.

The trash out there in the pitiful prairie remnant got me to thinking yesterday about whether or not any of it was worthwhile, even from the get-go. I think Lightheart and the others were right to protest, even if against overwhelming odds. I don't mean to celebrate "tilting at windmills." But how else will native birds and their habitats receive protection when they are jeopardized? How else will politicians and developers be put on notice that their decisions have real consequences?

I agree with the reputed views of a Populist agitator from the nineteenth century, who supposedly told a bunch of angry Kansans, "What you farmers need to do is raise less corn and more *Hell.*" I suppose that's what Lightheart had in mind when she climbed her mother tree—less shopping, more protecting.

Comfortable Longspurs

DECEMBER 27

Greetings from the snowy, iced-in portion of Arkansas, particularly Benton County and northeastern Oklahoma. Courtesy of Joe Woolbright and his four-wheel drive pick-up, I (we) managed a tour through the deep freeze on December 27. Main roads mostly clear, side roads mostly ice, mostly packed snow; most side-road ditches with obvious tire tracks and a few marooned vehicles. Lots of farmers hauling hay to cattle.

I was hoping for a Rough-legged Hawk, but saw none. Lots of Bald Eagles, as usual for this time, plus a few dark morph Harlan's Hawks, stark against the white landscape. North of Maysville proper, along Wet Prairie Road, a few American Tree Sparrows mixed with large flocks of White-crowned Sparrows, plus one Harris's Sparrow. Woolbright spotted a big flock of small brown birds, flying low over a stubble field: ~150 Lapland Longspurs. I just felt sure we'd soon have a Merlin behind them, but their movement seemed to be spurred by low flying Rock Pigeons (anyone out there ever been decoyed by them . . . I have), then a kestrel. They kept landing and taking off on what appeared to be a seed pile, near the road. Twenty meadowlarks paid no attention to pigeons or kestrel, as far as I could see. A small mixed species blackbird flock (including Rusty, Brewer's and Red-wings) came and went. We had a male and female Brewer's together, atop the seed pile, fine winter site, stark against white.

Woolbright generously parked so that I would have the longspur side. My scope on the window, I was digiscoping at close range, with 30–40 longspurs packed into each view. If you have experienced the joys (?) of standing out in the icy fields of December-January, watching the back-and-forth wheeling of longspurs flocks and wishing they would settle close, so you could see if they are ALL Laps, or what, and then settle for just distant views—all *tews* and rattles but no close views—you'll know right where I'm coming from. Joe Woolbright's truck with its warm, comfortable seat, open window opposite the wind: these were the most comfortable longspurs of my birding life.

From his side of the truck, Woolbright watched the longspur scene

A hungry flock of Lapland Longspurs north of Maysville on December 27, 2009. We always look for laps in big fields in harsh winter weather. They blend well into the landscape and can be hard to see unless we get very close.

for a healthy few minutes, but as things dragged on he began to complain of "sparrow neck." I wanted "just a few more images" to count and recount the constantly forming and reforming flock(s). And what about that possible Chestnut-collared Longspur? Woolbright is a practical person; to alleviate sparrow neck, he took in some shut eye while I worked the flocks with my scope. On the way back, down Loux Road: 3 Harris's Sparrows at Carol Loux's feeder, with White-crowneds, House Sparrows, etc.

Later, at home in Fayetteville, even more comfortable longspurs: images on my computer monitor. So much life, so much energy packed into little colorful sparrows, so far from where they started. Holiday greetings from "laplands." Maybe they came all the way from Greenland, or the Aleutians (old name "Alaska Longspur"), or . . . ?

2010

Short-eared Owl Roost at Fayetteville

JANUARY 17

Andrew Scaboo, doctoral candidate at University of Arkansas-Fayetteville, has been watching a big field where up to 8 Northern Harriers have been roosting for at least the past few weeks. That is not big news in parts of Arkansas where harriers are usually numerous, but it is significant in northwest Arkansas, where in mid-winter we see none or at most a scattered bird or two. Leesia Marshall-Rosenberger, also a U of A doctoral student, followed up with the sighting of a Short-eared Owl in this same field on January 10. Subsequently, she, Andy, and others have counted as many as 6 flying owls at dusk. Prior to these sightings, we have had only local, sparse, and scattered Short-eared Owl records for more than a half-century. So, ornithologically-speaking, this is big news for us.

The habitat in use by harriers and owls is a low-lying, former Tallgrass Prairie field marked by impressive prairie mounds. We have been calling these seasonal wetlands; the areas between the mounds are wet from snow melt and retain shallow standing water. Though the field has been heavily fescued, it retains significant Tallgrass Prairie flora, including the chief grasses: Big Bluestem, Little Bluestem, Indian Grass, Switch Grass, and Cordgrass in broad patches. Other prairie forb and grass species are also visible, even at mid-winter. My assumption is that if this Tallgrass Prairie flora remains, the prairie small mammal community has survived. It would explain the attraction for harriers and Short-eared Owls. Habitat patches like this survive because they are literally "too wet to plow." It has become a very rare habitat in western Arkansas, and the loss makes its unfortunate contribution to rangewide declines in grassland birds.

The owl field is immediately east of Woolsey Wet Prairie, adjacent Fayetteville's Westside Wastewater Treatment plant. Habitat-wise, it looks exactly like Woolsey prior to the ongoing restoration efforts.

A group of us (including Leesia, Andy, Carolina Monteiro, Brandon Schmidt, and Jacque Brown) linked up last evening (January 17) to look for American Tree Sparrows at Woolsey (~50 in one singing flock!), then crossed Broyles Avenue to walk the owl field. We found 6 Short-eared Owls roosting on the side of a big prairie mound, out in the wide-open middle of the big field. So we got great looks at the birds. Jacque Brown collected fascinating images of flying owls. We discovered Tallgrass Prairie attributes that remain. It is as good as any I've seen in northwestern Arkansas.

At dusk we linked up with Sam Holschbach and Dan Scheiman, fresh from their birding loop through northwest Arkansas. A thin gray ground fog begin to form, but we could still see several Short-eared Owls working the old former prairie fields, gliding up and down among mounds. Overhead, in the dark sky, there was just a sliver of moon, and nearby, bright Jupiter, with three moons visible through the bins. There was just enough light to silhouette overhead flocks of Mallards (and probably shovelers and Gadwalls) as they flew into the shallow ponds and flooded grasslands at Woolsey Wet Prairie.

Doug James and Karen Rowe during Trumpeter Swan release at Holla Bend NWR on February 10, 2010. Led by Arkansas Game & Fish Commission, this release was part of an ongoing effort to rebuilt Trumpeter populations in Arkansas.

Close Encounter with Trumpeters

FEBRUARY 10

An astonishing bird day February 10, 2010, began when I went with Doug James to Holla Bend National Wildlife Refuge for the release of Iowa-reared Trumpeter Swans. Karen Rowe of Arkansas Game & Fish has been working with Iowa Department of Natural Resources to move Trumpeters to Arkansas. This is part of a daring experiment called reverse migration imprinting. The idea is that young swans will

Joe Neal holding a
Trumpeter Swan ready
for release at Holla Bend
NWR near Russellville on
February 10, 2010. *Photo
by Sue Pekel.*

use their instincts to return north for nesting and later, return south for the non-breeding season.

The ground was snow covered in Fayetteville when we left and snow covered at Holla Bend two hours later. I had my binoculars, but yikes (!) forgot my coat. Doug loaned me a light blanket, which I stuffed indecorously under my fuzzy shirt. When we got near the Arkansas River to the release site, Karen was rounding up folks to carry swans from cages to water's edge. I was soon honored by a close encounter with Trumpeters—twenty-five or thirty pounds of swan and its pleasantly warm down, in my arms.

You first must hold their feet tightly—web feet the size of my hands. You firmly hug 'em to keep that eight-foot wing span closed. Then there is the famous trumpet, a very, very long neck, with an anxious, intelligent dark-eyed creature winding it around your neck, over your head, serpent-like, watching all, honking and hissing, way, way ready for release. Even standing in the snow and coatless, I was quite warm and fully employed hanging on to my swan!

When Doug and I worked on the book *Arkansas Birds* in 1986, there had been no certain Trumpeter records for the state since the early 1900s. Due to efforts by folks like Karen, Iowa DNR, and others, Trumpeters are coming back. For example, the flock now wintering each year at Magness Lake is a frequent topic of interest among birders in Arkansas.

In tough times with lots of bad news, it is easy to feel, as Mark Twain put it, that we are just "the damned human race." Yet, 16 Trumpeters found their freedom in Arkansas yesterday. Maybe this is not a banner line for Fox News, but it fairly reflects our hopes and aspirations. We are willing to put our amazing brains to work to put right what, in the case of loss of our wintering Trumpeters, had in past years unintentionally gone wrong.

Hooray for the Despised Ones

MARCH 5

I was up at the Craig State Fish Hatchery (Centerton, Benton County) this morning. There is a big pond on the west end that has never held water very well, and it usually is pretty grassy. It was burned off recently, and the burn was found agreeable by several bird species, including one of the despised ones, *Molothrus ater,* better known as cowbird. A flock of maybe 250 (including one that is lecustic) were thoroughly enjoying themselves in the short black, no doubt because many seeds are exposed by such burns.

Sort of out of the blue in my head, I said, "Hooray for the despised ones." I'm not sure where this came from, but I enjoyed watching the cowbirds on the burn.

Maybe it's because I also know them as buffalo birds, their old name. I do not blame them individually or collectively for what our species has done to the landscape, leading to an explosion of cowbirds and the explosion of negative impacts (like, Black-capped Vireo decline caused by cowbird nest parasitism). In terms of the negatives we collectively despise as "cowbirds," please allow me to note that we are ourselves a bunch of cowbirds. What we see as so negative about *M. ater* is a reasonable reflection of what *Homo sapiens* have done, negatively speaking. So maybe a little understanding of *M. ater* could be a useful primer for us to better understand us, *H. sapiens*.

On another of the hated blackbirds front, there were at least two to three hundred Great-tailed Grackles around the dairy farms at Vaughn (just south of the hatchery). Today they were as shiny, purple, golden-eyed, and almost impossibly great-tailed, and constantly squeaking, clacking, whistling and generally strutting their stuff.

A Daffodil Day

MARCH 12

Northwest Arkansas Audubon Society has a field trip to the Shores Lake area of the Ozark National Forest on Saturday March 27. It will be led by Bill Beall, the veteran birder from Fort Smith who has birded this area for years, including big stands of native shortleaf pine. I went out there to look around today. It is one of the real gems in our part of the state.

I got to Shores Lake, not on I-540, but down old 71, then east on State 348 just south of Mountainburg. You get to the end of 348, then the highway assumes several local names; fear not! Just keep heading east. Old 71 and 348 provide a leisurely way to see the magnificent Boston Mountains. The sixteen miles from old 71 to Fern and Shores Lake wind and turn, climb and descend, both in elevation and in time. It looks pretty modern near Mountainburg, but further east and deeper into the hills is the feel and look of an older Arkansas : homes with big porches and yards full of old time varieties of simple flowering daffodils. The previous generations also set out yuccas and these grace many of the older yards. A big yard was full of migrating robins. A farm pond at Fern was all about spring peepers and Red-winged Blackbirds.

The huge shortleaf pine stands along 215 south of Fern hosted a flock of 9 Wild Turkeys, and many flocks of American Goldfinches. I'm sure I saw 200. There were goldfinches up in the small cones and goldfinches seeking tiny seeds in ripe sweetgum balls. A Sharp-shinned Hawk flew across the highway carrying prey about half the hawk's size. Pine Warblers are in full song. Eastern Towhees were *che-winking* in the thickets around timber harvest areas. Purple Finches were probing the newly blossomed tree flowers in the bottoms at Shores Lake. And a Barred Owl called from the ridge. Witch hazel was still in bloom along the creek at Shores Lake and later, also at Winslow along old 71.

Today it was just a little too early for Black-and-white Warblers and Louisiana Waterthrushes. Of course that didn't keep me from trying. I'll bet they'll be there on the twenty-seventh.

Folks in the Fort Smith area will probably take I-40 to Mulberry, then north on 215 to Shores Lake. This is a simple and straightforward path. Folks from Fayetteville-Springdale-Rogers could take I-540 to I-40, but I found the travel on old 71, then 348 and the various roads it becomes (Old Locke, etc.) to be a pleasurable beginning of a fun birding expedition. It is almost all paved (just a few miles in the middle are still gravel). I Googled-up a map showing this route, and I can email this to anyone who wants to go that way, or just type Shores Lake, Ozark National Forest into Google Earth.

We are going to meet up at the picnic area entrance on the west side of the lake. Just as you get to Shores Lake, notice the sign that indicates the left fork for "Shores Lake -1, Camping, White Rock 7." Meeting time is 9 a.m.

1P2, Watching:
Dardenelle and Holla Bend

MARCH 13

We met Kenny and LaDonna Nichols at Lake Dardenelle on March 13. Besides me: Carole Jones from Fayetteville, her buddy Kelly Chitwood and Kelly's friend Micki McIntyre. It was cool, gray, and windy, so before meeting up with Kenny, I had my scope set up inside the state park visitor's center, taking advantage of big panoramic windows overlooking Dardenelle. From the windless warmth inside, we had American Coots and long ways off Lesser Scaup appearing and disappearing in the day's white-caps. I was teasing Kenny about what a swell deal he had for spotting rare winter gulls when he mentioned that this was the SECOND time he'd ever been inside the building . . .

So, off we went toward the Delaware area, where midst gray cool and serious white-caps, we had an unmistakable Lesser Black-backed Gull cleanly perched on a much bird white-washed "Delaware" sign, Arkansas Nuclear One puffing in the background. Then Kenny found the second Lesser Black-backed Gull, this one a grayish plumaged juvenile that I had assumed was an immature Herring Gull. I wonder how many "Herring Gull" juveniles I've seen just upriver at Kerr Dam in Oklahoma? In the wind and in the gray cool, Kenny shared on-the-spot field ornithology, explaining the difference between Herring and Lesser Black-backed juvs. Gulls are an acquired taste.

Then to Holla Bend National Wildlife Refuge (nearby), which is where Kelly, who made the long drive from Camden, had wanted to go. In a shallow pool we had a male pintail, Green-winged Teals (~100), a few Blue-winged Teals, Gadwalls, a couple of shovelers, etc. There were also two Trumpeter Swans, with green neck collars. One of them was number 0P4. Number 1P2 seemed oblivious to us, its extraordinary neck and head tucked in apparent repose, BUT an image I collected shows that it was steadily watching the curious goings on (us) with dark eye almost hidden above an immaculate white back.

There were plenty of hawks on the refuge. One in particular, hundreds of yards away across an open field, lead to controversy. So what hawk, very rare in Arkansas and strongly associated with the open windy country, is at distance white looking with a dark belly band? Of course I shouted out ROUGH LEGGED! Ominously, I heard no amen from Kenny, who also had a scope on it, and there was no amen from LaDonna, who was intelligently in the truck out of the wind, holding her little dog, Missy, with a full view of proceedings. Nobody else had amened, either, but it would be such a very good bird . . .

Its legs were unfeathered (Kenny), but I think maybe feathered (me). Look at that tail with the wide black band (me); silence on the Kenny front. I just love these long-ways-away birds, because they permit so much room for fantasy . . . then the bird flew . . . its complete association with the tribe of light morph or juvenile Red-tailed Hawks was decently or indecently (me) evident.

On the way out: hundreds of Ring-billed Gulls perching on freshly turned soil, others closely and rather artistically following the plow. In the same field, ~75 Rusty Blackbirds, my highest count of the year.

Unintended Binocular Acceleration

MARCH 14

Jacque Brown, David Oakley, and I toured the broad agricultural fields of the Arkansas River Valley today. We started out in Oklahoma at Dora and Moffett, crossed into Arkansas at Fort Smith and continued on through Van Buren to Frog Bayou Wildlife Management Area and the Alma sewer ponds. At Moffett we were much taken by a mixed species goose flock that included Canada (26), Ross's (1), Snow (6 white, 6 blues), and White-fronted (1). No less fascinating: a line-up of four cars from the Bonnie and Clyde era, rusting gracefully with trees growing through broken windows, silently proclaiming glories of the Nash Rambler and Ford coupe.

American Pipits (33) patrolled smooth turf just east of Van Buren. We were able to find a legal spot to peep at the posted glories of Hollis Lake: Canvasback (5), American White Pelican (15), Wood Ducks,

American Wigeon, Ring-necked Duck, Gadwall, a few Mallards—ALL flushed suddenly by a subadult Bald Eagle. A Red-tailed Hawk carried a HUGE snake away from the highway ditch.

We continued to drift slowly east through the bottoms, traveling a well potholed farm road. I was much taken by small groups of Horned Larks in 5 places, and I had my window open to hopefully hear more. So I hear another squeak—it must be a lark?—and the Toyota bounced free and clear across the mother-of-all-potholes. I looked around and saw Jacque's head lurch forward and her Bushnell Legend binoculars simultaneously lurch upward, then rapidly reverse, a perfectly choreographed and wholly unintended binocular acceleration. Eyepieces were crammed into her eyeballs, then suddenly out again, and her head ended up against the headrest, no worse for wear, Thank Goodness!

I guess Jacque could sue me for negligence or Toyota for bad springs, or perhaps Bushnell for failure to install devices that inhibit unintended binocular acceleration, and include pothole-making Crawford County farmers in the complaint. We three held a quick powwow just east of Lake Pothole and decided that Bushnell might need to install a cheap fix for the binocular strap to slow forward momentum and pad eyepieces. The manufacturer's recall will no doubt be forthcoming.

The Horned Lark vocalization that precipitated the unintended binocular acceleration turned out actually to be a squeaky steering column in my 1991 Toyota, a defect that showed up at 247,000 miles of such rural Arkansas adventure. Jacque and David aren't the only ones who have noticed this squeak, but this is the first time I've thought it a Horned Lark in flight. The unintended binocular acceleration was also a first. Somewhere in this discussion, David Oakley collapsed into a laughing hysteria, and he dragged Jacque and I down with him, enough that we could barely pay attention to Savannah Sparrows in the plowed fields and the sudden dramatic flash of a male Northern Harrier.

As most good ones do, this birding expedition ended at or near a sewer pond. At Alma, we could just barely make out a nice flock of Lesser Scaup (38), very sharp-looking in the treated wastewater. On several farm ponds right across the road, Blue-winged Teal (8, 14) were amazing and truly immaculate in their smart fresh plumage, returned from the south, all about spring refreshment.

Birds in the Black

MARCH 17

Northwest Arkansas Audubon Society continues to find its way back from its state of near dissolution in fall 2008. Many hands came forward to save it then. Some have since departed. By my calculation, more than half of the current board has changed. I've been thinking about this, especially, because Scott Michaud, who set up a web site for the reorganized NWAAS, is returning to Maryland. He wanted to see Greater Prairie-Chickens before he left, so we traveled over to the Tallgrass Prairie Preserve yesterday.

One of the first birds we spotted was a Rough-legged Hawk (light morph type), but it is late in the season, and it was the only one we saw. We did not see Sprague's Pipit or Smith's Longspur. What we did have were wonderful views of birds foraging widely in burned grasslands.

The first bison we encountered were foraging on young grasses pushing up from the black. Right there among them, and all around, Killdeer. We traveled miles along burned grasslands, and there were Killdeer everywhere, staging or pausing in migration and spread out like American Robins in a shortgrass pasture. It reminded me of a small American Golden-Plover flock I saw a few years ago. They were using a blackened, recently burned part of Chesney Prairie Natural Area. There were also robins all over these burned areas, pausing in their northward push.

Grasslands along Sand Creek had also been burned. We saw several flocks of Harris's Sparrows foraging in the blackened grasses. Their dark face masks blended quite well with the blackened habitat, though of course, I can't say the same for their pink bills! Brewer's Blackbirds and Brown-headed Cowbirds foraged the black, too, all but disappearing unless in flight.

One of the great miracles of the modern age is the cell phone. Scott and his wife Amy were still working out details with a mover. In one of the places where we hoped for prairie-chickens, we had to hold up a bit while Scott handled a cell call from the mover. So here we are out in the middle of the prairie. Scott has his binoculars employed scanning fields

Female Red-winged Blackbird with food for nestlings in a small cat tail–lined marshy spot near Centerton on June 18, 2006.

as he talks to a mover. I'm watching great billows of smoke from the prescribed burn to our east, listening to the distant tap-tap of oil wells, the closer songs of chorus frogs and singing Eastern Meadowlarks, the feel of the wind, the sweep of a flock of Red-winged Blackbirds, and a Greater Yellowlegs that suddenly flushes from a pond below us. Scott's call finished, we scan the big shallow pond and see Canvasback (1), Green-winged Teal (10), and Mallards (2).

We did not see the chickens. On my last trip over here (in January), I saw over 50. I guess unpredictability is part of what keeps birding interesting. I'm sorry Scott didn't see them, but I'm glad they know how and when to blend into their landscape.

Richard Stauffacher has agreed to fill in behind Scott as NWAAS webmaster. Richard is an artist who has included depictions of local birds and plants in his etchings. I knew he could be a good webmaster for NWAAS because his own website, etchings.org, is well-organized and user-friendly.

Good luck, Scott and Amy. Welcome Richard.

Real Teal

MARCH 21

Geology I enjoy involves what we see and how it got that way, a distant past imagined. Massive road cuts through once scenic mountains become opportunities to study the earth's ancient history, rock layer after exposed rock layer.

On March 20, 2010, I'm thinking about this and migrating ducks, at the edge of a pond, in a cold rain with some sleet mixed and big snow promised, behind Wal-Mart near I-540 in Benton County. I saw ducks on the pond while driving. I finally figured out how to get near them. Now, crouching under a golf umbrella, with cover provided by last year's blackberry thicket, I have views of Canada Goose (2), Wood Duck (3), Gadwall (4), Mallard (2), Blue-winged Teal (8), Northern Shoveler (30), Green-winged Teal (5), Bufflehead (2), Pied-billed Grebe (5), American Coot (4), and 16 Ring-billed Gulls; in short, a small pond big with ducks and water birds.

These migrants are held up in their northward journey by a storm. I'm old enough to remember a past with celebrations of the vernal equinox here in the Ozarks of western Arkansas featuring snow up to the blooming daffodils. Now we have another. Today my yard is a white plain polka-dotted by yellow trumpets.

In honor of this spring gift, I'm trying an angle novel for me on duck migration. Instead of endless jeremiads of frustration against "growth" and "development" and the destruction of all nature straight and true, I'm determined to think like a geologist: imagine the way it was and see how we can go forward.

Back before our kind began our plunder in the 1820s, Blue-winged Teal had fewer choices to rest and loaf as they headed north through here. There were no true ponds and no lakes. Our grasslands in the western Arkansas Ozarks did have extensive low areas whose clay-rich soils held water. So around the vernal equinox, when came big rains and occasional deep wet snow, these low fields held scattered shallow pools of water, forming playas. Here's where teal and their brethren weathered a spring storm.

In cold and sleet out behind Walmart and 540, I'm imagining how our landscape serves migrating teal, even as we plunder on. For northwest Arkansas, we could include the shallows of Lake Fayetteville and many other area lakes, older farm ponds midst open grasslands, the concentration of sixteen fish ponds at the state hatchery in Centerton—all that sort of thing. Shallow pools created at Woolsey Wet Prairie in Fayetteville have been much favored by teal. The success of Woolsey—a project funded as mitigation for wetland loss—has spurred interest elsewhere in northwest Arkansas, as more natural habitat is lost to "growth" and "development," and planners seek opportunities to mitigate the ongoing habitat plunder.

These are some thoughts for the vernal equinox. As in the much distant past, there are Blue-winged Teal passing through western Arkansas and, thank goodness, many places to view them. A big old farm pond behind Walmart is not as romantic as a rain and snow filled playa, but the real teal are out there, resplendent in spring plumage, indomitable in their quest for the future.

The Power of Prayer

MARCH 28

The great rarity of Brown-headed Nuthatches in the western Ozarks intrigued me thirty years ago while working on the book *Arkansas Birds* with Doug James. Bill Beall, a University of Arkansas-Fayetteville business student back in Doug's early teaching days, has been the only person to regularly find these nuthatches in the western Ozarks. Both nuthatch and required habitat—extensive stands of mature shortleaf pine— were once widespread in the Ozarks. Bill, now treasurer for Northwest Arkansas Audubon Society, led a field trip into his nuthatch kingdom on March 27. Nobody but Bill and Doug had ever seen a Brown-headed Nuthatch in the western Ozarks, so we were pretty excited. Maybe twenty-five folks were present at the start. It was a wonderfully eclectic group from all over northwest Arkansas, Fort Smith north through Fayetteville to Benton County including Siloam Springs in the west, and even one woman from Missouri.

The rough Boston Mountains section of the Ozark National Forest around Fern and Shores Lake (northern Franklin County) contains some awe-inspiring and well-managed shortleaf pine forests. We birded around Shores Lake without too much excitement: Purple Finches, an uncommonly good look at a red Fox Sparrow, a chorus of Fish Crows recently arrived in the Ozarks, and campers with loud music who turned it down for us. Then we moved south, toward Fern, and began a process of birding the better looking pine stands. It was pretty windy and Neotropical migrants all but absent. We enjoyed numerous Pine Warblers and got great looks, BUT no Black-and-white, no Yellow-throated Vireo, or gnatcatcher.

Serviceberries are blooming everywhere and wildflowers too, but no Brown-headed Nuthatch. As we moved into early afternoon, my mind was drifting some. What a field trip: we had Doug James, a founder of Arkansas Audubon Society and its first and longest serving curator, two past presidents of Arkansas Audubon Society (Bill and Sandy Berger), plus the current president and vice president of NWAAS (Doug and Joanie Patterson) and LOTS of persistence. Around 2:30,

Brown-headed
Nuthatch is a rare
bird in mature pines
near Fern in the Ozark
National Forest.

Bill stopped us in front of the last pine stand of the day. He calls this "a hail Mary stop." We were parked on highway 215, south of Fern. Also, we were stopped right in front of a broken pine stub with a tiny hole. Suddenly, wonderfully, we had one Brown-headed Nuthatch in a tree adjacent the cavity tree, and another looked quickly from within. So there was the day's story: lack of results in other stops was likely due in part to the birds being quiet while nesting. We did not resolve distribution and abundance questions, but we may return when noisy family groups are about. Jacque Brown and David Oakley collected fine images of these rare birds of the western Ozarks.

Now we are off to the second part of the trip: Arkansas River Valley around Dyer and Alma. We miss a huge rain storm, "duck" through Frog Bayou WMA (Blue-winged Teal, Northern Shoveler, etc.) and then ON to the Alma sewer ponds for hopefully Black-bellied Whistling-Ducks. None at the sewer ponds, BUT across the road, *Plegadis* ibis (2) with Blue-winged Teal, American Wigeon, etc. A couple of Rough-winged Swallows work with the wind. Now we get to the last pond (which sounds like the last mature pine stand); 17 Great-tailed Grackles squeak and whistle in a far tree. Helpful local law enforcement worry, politely, about our parked cars. Then, as Bill expected, we have fine views of Black-bellied Whistling Ducks (45 on one pond).

My original posting to ARBIRD-L on this field trip was entitled, "Brown-headed Nuthatches in the Western Ozarks," but only because I was afraid my preferred title would stir up the anxiety termed "the cultural wars." So I also left out the following events, also part of the day.

It was maybe around noon, or thereabouts, as we experienced a fair dry spell on birds generally, and a total drought on Brown-headed Nuthatches in particular, I looked up in the front seat and saw that Bill's wife Toka was pretty busy with something . . . but I wasn't sure what. For one thing, she was getting a chocolate chip cookie out of a bag for me. But that wasn't all. When I asked, she said she was praying for nuthatches. I thought she was kidding, so I asked again. She confirmed it. So I asked, jokingly, if she believed it of value to pray for a good price on a used car. She confirmed that, too, and Bill amened as well, both on the price of a used car AND especially for nuthatches.

In my birding experiences I have prayed that my old Toyota would start when we were out in the middle of nowhere, and that my even older legs would get me across a huge field that might have Smith's Longspurs, or maybe, hopefully, Greater Prairie-Chickens, but I've never prayed for Brown-headed Nuthatches. We eventually got them, and considering how we did, the events at least exhibit the look and shape of a miracle.

They Got Away

APRIL 8

We had a brief rain and cool front in northwest Arkansas, so yesterday (April 6) I went over to Chesney Prairie Natural Area. My first stop was the curlew field just northwest of Chesney. The field is wet; there are plenty of Savannah Sparrows along the road, but only a few Killdeer in the field. Next stop was Chesney, with focus on the twenty acres recently burned in the Couch unit. I had great close looks at a lone American Golden-Plover, flushed 2 Upland Sandpipers, 4 Killdeer, and 20 + Savannah Sparrows, plus some other stuff (White-crowned, Barn Swallow, etc.).

My drive home takes me by Siloam Springs Airport. About midway, a tight flock of 10 shore birds made a low pass, apparently headed to the old mounded prairie fields there. I first thought golden-plover, then probably Upland Sandpiper, but not Killdeer. A truck was on my bumper and I couldn't properly execute that emergency ID stop the situation demanded. Thus, even my justifiably infamous harum-scarum stopping couldn't be deployed, including the parachute attached to the rear window of my trusty ole Toyota, space shuttle-like in its stopping power and in support of unexpected events with potential excellence (?) in field ornithology.

So they got away un-IDed. What a shame. I woke this morning with that tight flock on my mind. Now it must be filed in that burgeoning cabinet of what-was-its. Hope none of yours are getting away.

Even with Rain and Buffalo Gnats

APRIL 24

Jacque Brown, David Oakley, and I dodged rain showers all morning April 24, but still managed to bird Cheery (Cherry) Bend and Cass in the Ozark National Forest along the Pig Trail (Highway 23). We got the resident birds hoped for (but only a few species of transients): Broad-winged Hawk, Wood Thrush, Blue-winged Warbler, Northern Parula, Yellow-throated Warbler, Black-throated Green Warbler, Prairie Warbler, Cerulean Warbler, Black-and-white Warbler, Worm-eating Warbler, Ovenbird, Louisiana Waterthrush, Kentucky Warbler, Hooded Warbler, Scarlet Tanager, Rose-breasted Grosbeak, Baltimore Oriole, etc.

We did not encounter substantial fallout associated with the through transients (e.g. Golden-winged Warbler). This is perhaps a week away or so.

The Black-throated Green Warbler was a brilliant male at the Cherry Bend parking area for the Ozark Highlands Trail crossing of Highway 23. This former campground overlooks a deep ravine, providing views of tree canopies at eye level. We had the singing bird in such trees, below which were blooming the brilliant pinks of our native

Three photographers at Eagle Watch Nature Trail June 19, 2010: Terry Stanfill (striped shirt), Jacque Brown, and David Oakley. They have contributed to documenting the ornithological wealth of northwestern Arkansas.

azeleas. The colors of the bird, trees, azeleas, and wild roiling sky were staggering. We had another such view of a small flock (5 birds) of male Baltimore Orioles, attired in smart spring plumage, all orange and black against the radiant spring green of a rainy day at Fly Gap.

Log trucks, Harleys, and tightly packed pods of passenger vehicles periodically wound and roared and groaned around tight twists and turns of Highway 23. The hurry in such situations is really evident when you are on foot. A few slowed for three strangely attired ones (us) looking intently at a Cerulean Warbler. I have been in the cars, in a hurry, racing through life for somewhere (?), arriving, then racing somewhere else (!). I was pleased to be on the ground today, one of the elect ones viewing the male Cerulean. There is a time and place in life where hurry is unavoidable. I'm thankful it was my opportunity yesterday afoot, even with rain and (see below).

The only bad (?) was buffalo gnats. To quote Walter Anderson, they were "terrific." These are black flies, small creatures all about blood sucking. I think their scientific handle is *Cnephia pecuarum,* the southern buffalo gnat. They swarmed us all day. When I got home, part of my left hand was swollen with bites, and I had itchy welts all over the back of my neck and head. My impression, though, is that lots of buffalo gnats equals good birds.

Not sure there is any quantitative support for that idea, but these upland forests of the Boston Mountains are full of Neotropical song-birds and on a rainy day in spring, buffalo gnats.

Prairie Dowitchers

MAY 14

Thank god for walleyes, and I don't say that as a fisherman, but rather as a birder. Every year around the first and second weeks of May, personnel at Craig State Fish Hatchery in Centerton drain ponds to catch walleyes for release in area lakes. Fresh drained pond flats are shorebird stopover magnets.

That's why I was there on May14, despite a nasty weather report with angry knots of lightning/thunder/heavy rain moving through. I was watching a few birds on such a pond as big thunder boomed and lightning streaked—and lo, suddenly—curtains of downpours visibly on the way—the pond flat received 20 breeding dressed Stilt Sandpipers and 8 similarly attired dowitchers.

A big thunder clap and lightning bolt startled us all. The birds bounced up and many left for another pond, except the dowitchers. As the rain intensified, they oriented themselves directly into the northeast wind, bills like weather vanes, raised slightly above horizontal. The pond was swept by huge hard raindrops. Dowitchers closed their eyes and re-oriented their beaks as the storm moved over. We waited.

We get both dowitcher species at Centerton during this time. Centerton is part of the former Tallgrass Prairie of northwest Arkansas, and I am especially curious about the Short-billed Dowitcher subspecies *hendersoni* that breeds in the prairie provinces of Canada. For this I have poured through the shorebird books looking for the key, that salient

Willet flock at Centerton on April 28, 2005. Willets and many other shorebird species made a brief but dramatic stopover in northwest Arkansas during a huge spring storm that slowed the pace of northward migration.

detail, to reliably separate breeding dressed long-bills and short-bills. But I'm still no good at it.

The tried and true method of separating the two species is listening to calls. So as the storm passes, I pull on my muck boots and head out. Soon I have *tu-tu-tu* calls of short-bills. At home, looking at my poor images, I would say they do look like birds headed for nesting in the prairie provinces.

Chesney

MAY 15

We were all decked-out in our raingear for the Chesney Prairie Natural Area field trip May 15. We had a three-inch rain the evening before and

Land steward Joe Woolbright with Big Bluestem Grass at Chesney Prairie Natural Area on August 14, 2004. This Siloam Springs native has taken on management of Tallgrass Prairie habitat in western Arkansas for Arkansas Natural Heritage Commission.

80+% predicted for more. We had our birding mojo workin'—three hours of NO rain and LOTS of birds.

My anticipation is always keen before a Chesney trip because it is a remnant of a once widespread Tallgrass Prairie ecosystem. I always expect the old prairie to rise from the dead Lazarus-like. That's called optimism.

Northern Bobwhite—two different areas had birds. Red-headed Woodpecker—two birds defending snags, apparently with success, from starlings. Willow Flycatcher—gone from most of Arkansas, but always at Chesney as a migrant. Will it finally nest at Chesney? We had satisfying views of this bird giving *fitz-bew!* calls as it foraged around a blackberry-sumac thicket in an area burned two years ago. Bell's Vireo—once common in northwestern Arkansas, now rare and local. The habitat consists of shrubs (rough-leafed dogwood, indigo bush, sumac, etc.) typical of the former prairies. We've had breeding-season birds at Chesney before. There was also one at nearby Stump Prairie, now really blazing with flowering indigo bush. Savannah Sparrow—the end of a long winter sojourn is at hand for them and I saw a total of 6 birds (in twos, so paired?) along the road leading to Chesney and as they migrate north, toward the future. Blue Grosbeak—typical bird of open grasslands. Painted Bunting—1 or 2 birds; the one we saw was one of the first year males. Dickcissel—in the fields and singing away. Orchard Oriole—may still be migrating through, since we saw quite a few, but at least one pair was building a nest. American Goldfinch—small bright groups all over, I guess awaiting thistles. Quite a few migrants, too: Mourning Warbler, American Redstart, Wilson's Warbler, Alder Flycatcher, Lincoln's Sparrow, etc.

This prairie is certainly a remnant, but it is rising. Vegetative management fostering a habitat mosaic supports species with diverse needs. In a single year, part of the area is burned, others are left for burning in a different year. It's all accessible via the trail system. One of the tough things about learning prairies is just trying to walk through them in the growing season. The birding and botanizing community can thank Joe Woolbright, who generously got out on a busy rainy week and re-mowed all of the trails through Chesney.

Mississippi Kites at Fayetteville on May 25, 2010. Ricky Corder noticed these birds while commuting to work and shared his discovery on ARBIRD-L. We subsequently found a nest under construction, the first documented for northwest Arkansas.

Suspicious Activity— Mississippi Kites, Fayetteville

MAY 25

Ricky Corder has made several posts about Mississippi Kites in northeastern Fayetteville he has been seeing on his way to work. I know seeing kites is no big deal to folks in parts of the state where they are expected and common, but "expected and common" is not the case in the Ozarks of northwestern Arkansas. This is only the second time since the 1980s that kites have been seen in late May, and the other record involved a single bird. Ricky's involves two adults, together. Pretty suspicious.

The birds today were perched together in a snag, along a busy connector (Skillern Road) that is just east of the old Skillern farmhouse. The snag is actually within the gated and very walled-off Savanna Estates development, but easily visible from Skillern, a public road.

I contacted Ricky and got some more information about his sightings, then went out there this morning, driving slowly and carefully as I could on Skillern, pulling into driveways and such to let traffic pass and to scan the sky and treetops. I saw a box turtle on the road and moved it while I searched. Also, before actually finding Ricky's kites, I noticed Savanna Estates and its Neighborhood Watch—"WE REPORT ALL SUSPICIOUS ACTIVITY TO THE POLICE—and the added comment "ACTIVELY IN FORCE," etc.

This stuff always makes me laugh, since I live in a part of Fayetteville in which EVERYTHING looks suspicious. There isn't enough law enforcement in the entire county to keep track. Then I joked to myself, "I wonder if Neighborhood Watch has reported kites for THEIR suspicious (possibly sexual) activity?"

It did occur to me, albeit v-e-r-y briefly, that looking for kites, not to mention turtle relocation, might be viewed as suspicious activity of a different kind and bring forth the forces of law'n order. Of course it did. I had collected a bunch of images of the perched kites (from Skillern) before the Fayetteville Police Department showed. But this still leaves us with the suspicious activity by the kites.

Pelicans

MAY 26

I'm just back from a fun day of birding. I drove across Fayetteville, found Mississippi Kites, collected a bunch of images, then headed home. Had a call about some other kites, so drove to another spot, but didn't find any. Out of the car, and home at last, in time for the news: lots on the oil spill.

I have a very cool little art book of drawings called *Pelicans*. Line drawings of Brown Pelicans by Walter Inglis Anderson are at the book's core. The story of her father's art and these particular drawings is presented by Mary Anderson Pickard. It's about mangroves, Brown Pelicans, frigate birds, fiddler crabs in mangroves, and one man's celebration.

Mary writes, "In the late 1940s and 50s, Anderson reveled in the

American White Pelicans at Lake Sequoyah on November 10, 2008. Pelicans stop during fall migration in the lake's shallow waters.

'tremendously musical harmonies' of thousands of nesting pelicans in the Chandeleur rookeries on North Key . . ."

The Chandeleur Islands, off the Louisiana coast—that's where the oil is ashore now. That's where they're getting the images of oiled eggs, oiled nestlings, and adult pelicans diving in oiled water.

A few years after these drawings, Walter Anderson began to notice the decline in nesting Brown Pelicans. No one then understood DDT. Anderson passed away in 1963, a year after the publication of the alarm bell *Silent Spring* by Rachael Carson.

He did not live to see the bitter fight over banning DDT and the subsequent slow return of pelicans to the Chandeleurs. Nor did he live to see the pelicans return so strongly that just last year, they were removed from the list of endangered species. His drawings remain. They remind us in a timely fashion.

I doubt blame will get us very far on this one, for we are all implicated. I think Anderson was onto something in honoring "tremendously musical harmonies." It seems a useful goal as these agonies play out and we try to figure out where we go from here.

Lesser Yellowlegs at Centerton on August 20, 2004. These shorebirds are common transients in open areas with shallow water.

Yellowlegs Not So Yellow?
Oiled Birds in Arkansas?

MAY 28

Since the big deep sea oil well blowout off coastal Louisiana is directly south of us, I assume we may see a fair number of partially oiled birds in Arkansas starting in mid-summer, as surviving waders and other species nesting along the Gulf Coast, barrier islands, and deeper waters impacted by oil make their annual post-breeding northward dispersal. I also assume that if a significant amount of oil remains in the Gulf environment, we will see partially oil birds next spring.

I did a very quick and dirty estimation on what we might just see in northwest Arkansas, and I came up with a very rough number of 65 species likely to pass through the oil that we would normally expect up here. I also assume the only birds we are likely to see are those only moderately oiled (heavily oiled birds perish). That is, we may see yellowlegs with legs not so yellow, etc. Considered statewide, the number would be much higher.

Wouldn't it make sense to try and track this statewide in the coming year? I am not sure exactly how we could do this, but folks could post their oiled bird sightings to ARBIRD-L, as they did storm birds (Sooty Terns, etc.) after Gustav in September 2008. Bird photographers could provide direct evidence. Keeping track of this some way or another could help us understand collateral damage associated with such disasters.

I know there is a lot more to this, but it doesn't seem too soon to start thinking about how we might contribute to understanding the broad temporal and geographic impacts.

A Slow Creek Walk
and a Loud *Pee Ur Wee*

JUNE 27

This afternoon I took a slow creek walk in the shallows of West Fork (of the White River) south of Fayetteville. It was a lazy Sunday with space for birding, botanizing, watching fish, small snakes, and crawfish in the shallows. It would be HOT but for a steady south breeze and enormous cloud caravans heading across the known (and unknown!) universe and turning glare into pleasing patterns of black shade and slanted light. It's intoxicating—luxuriant wealthy combination of humid soil, warm flowing water, breathing plants large and small, and the blessing of time to enjoy it all.

In one spot there were a couple of low piles of flat rocks monumenting a recent bout of sitting and fishing. Adjacent, a long fallen sycamore limb covered with white splatter provided evidence of a different angler (I'm thinking kingfisher).

I had a Wood Thrush and Yellow-throated Warbler singing at the old bridge, along with a bunch of others: Northern Parula, Red-eyed Vireo, Indigo Bunting, etc. Along the shady woods just above the creek: great spreading blue masses of tall bellflower, thickets of wild hydrangea, dense stands of the grass called inland sea oats, and another of my favorite grasses: bottlebrush. I kept hearing sharp *chinks* of a Louisiana Waterthrush and finally saw it in one of the bellflower thickets—so maybe a late nest? Or young birds hiding?

Back in the days before I had a car, I did most of my birding on a bicycle. This worked pretty well because the West Fork is conveniently only a few miles from Fayetteville's center. It flows through farmland and forested hills, and Tilly Willy Road follows the creek for quite a ways. The country road is lightly traveled and perfect for bicycling. I have seen runners out here, too. Tilly Willy is an old name. It has a newer fancy name, but I can't even remember it.

Up in the woods I hear rolling whistles of a Summer Tanager. Right along the road: the curious, curly, peeling of shagbark hickories now with lots of nuts. Suddenly, darting across in front of me, an Eastern Wood-Pewee. And maybe, just so I don't miss the ID, a nice loud *pee ur wee*.

APPENDIX
Birding Places in Northwest Arkansas

BENTON COUNTY 1–10

1. Centerton
2. Beaty Prairie, Maysville
3. Chesney Prairie Natural Area, Siloam Springs
4. Round Prairie, Cherokee City
5. Eagle Watch Nature Trail, Gentry
6. Pea Ridge National Military Park
7. Lake Atalanta, Rogers
8. Slate Gap and Lost Bridge on Beaver Lake
9. Wedington, Ozark National Forest
10. Hobbes State Park Conservation Area and Rocky Branch

CARROLL COUNTY 11–14

11. Beaver Lake Dam
12. Lake Leatherwood, Eureka Springs
13. Berryville
14. Ninestone Land Trust

BOONE COUNTY 15

15. Baker Prairie Natural Area, Harrison

WASHINGTON COUNTY 9, 16–20

9. Wedington, Ozark National Forest
16. Springdale

17. Lake Fayetteville, Wilson Springs, University farm, Woolsey Wet Prairie, Fayetteville
18. Lake Sequoyah
19. Devil's Den State Park
20. Bob Kidd Lake, Prairie Grove

MADISON COUNTY 21–22

21. Prairie Township, Hindsville
22. Huntsville

NEWTON COUNTY 23–25

23. Boxley, Cave Mountain, Upper Buffalo River
24. Ponca
25. Jasper

CRAWFORD COUNTY 26–28

26. Frog Bayou WMA, Arkansas River
27. Alma
28. Mulberry, Mulberry River

FRANKLIN COUNTY 29–32

29. Cherry Bend
30. Cass, Redding Campground, Ozark NF
31. Shores Lake
32. White Rock

JOSEPH NEAL is a native of western Arkansas. He is co-author of *Arkansas Birds* (with Douglas A. James) and wrote the historical section for *History of Washington County Arkansas.* He has worked as a biologist for three decades, including 17 years in the USDA Forest Service as a wildlife biologist working to restore the endangered Red-cockaded Woodpecker in the Ouachita Mountains. Now retired from the Forest Service, he continues his Arkansas bird studies from his home in Fayetteville. He is active in both Arkansas Audubon Society, where he is Curator of Bird Records, and Northwest Arkansas Audubon Society, where he serves as field trip leader. He writes and records commentaries for "Ozarks at Large," a feature on KUAF, a local National Public Radio affiliate. He is a Visiting Scholar in the University of Arkansas's Department of Biological Sciences and writes a local bird column for the *Washington County Observer.*

CPSIA information can be obtained at www.ICGtesting.com

235491LV00001B/143/P